Robert Roberts

Prophecy and The Eastern Question

Being an Exhibition of the Light Shed by the Scriptures of Truth

Robert Roberts

Prophecy and The Eastern Question
Being an Exhibition of the Light Shed by the Scriptures of Truth

ISBN/EAN: 9783337249427

Printed in Europe, USA, Canada, Australia, Japan

Cover: Foto ©Lupo / pixelio.de

More available books at **www.hansebooks.com**

PROPHECY

AND

The Eastern Question:

BEING

AN EXHIBITION OF THE LIGHT SHED BY THE SCRIPTURES OF TRUTH

ON THE MATTERS INVOLVED IN

THE CRISIS THAT HAS ARRIVED IN EASTERN AFFAIRS,

SHOWING

THE APPROACHING FALL OF THE OTTOMAN EMPIRE; WAR BETWEEN ENGLAND AND RUSSIA; THE SETTLEMENT OF THE JEWS IN SYRIA UNDER BRITISH PROTECTORATE;

The Appearing of Christ, the Infliction of Divine Vengeance on Mankind and

THE SETTING-UP OF THE KINGDOM OF GOD.

BY ROBERT ROBERTS,

(Of BIRMINGHAM.)

LONDON: F. PITMAN, 20, PATERNOSTER ROW.

BIRMINGHAM: R. ROBERTS, ATHENÆUM ROOMS, TEMPLE ROW.

1877.

PROPHECY AND THE EASTERN QUESTION.

CHAPTER I.

Public alarm at the Eastern Question—The political possibilities involved in it—Popular fears about prophecy—The reality of the foundation of them—Educated aversion to the subject unreasonable—The facts of the case—Human action under Divine guidance—Historic illustrations— First clue to the Eastern Question—God's purpose in the Holy Land— His promise to Abraham—The question of fulfilment considered.

THE Eastern Question has once again obtruded itself upon universal attention, with the effect of widespread public alarm. The sentiment of commiseration on behalf of the unhappy inhabitants of Bulgaria, aroused by the recital of the barbarities perpetrated among them by the Turks, has already given place to an uneasy apprehension that Russia may turn the opportunity to account for her own advantage, by making an assault, under cover of the popular indignation, upon the tottering edifice of Ottoman power, and acquire possession of Constantinople and the splendid territories so long desolated by the Turk. What this would mean, as regards the interests of Britain, is gravely known to all who have weighed the matter in all its bearings. It would be a menace to British power in India, and to menace that power would be to put in jeopardy the position, and ultimately the very existence of Britain in the world. The strange vicissitudes of history justify this view as involving at least a possible eventuality. Russia may be poor if we measure her resources by the requirements of British population; but she is a giant notwithstanding. She commands an army ten times the size of the British army, composed of hardy and hearty men, united by the enthusiasm of a common creed and faith in destiny. Politically, she is strengthened by the virtual alliance of Austria and Germany, who command between them 2,000,000 of armed men. Consequently, the possibility of war between Russia and England is regarded with great and just apprehensiveness by all classes of English people; and the future is regarded with something akin to a feeling of dread—a feeling reflected in the depressed state of all the institutions of the country.

But there is another element in the case which adds to the perturbation of public feeling, and imparts a peculiar solemnity to the crisis which is now engaging the thoughts of men ; it is the feeling that is abroad that these impending events have something to do with prophecy—that programme of divine operations on earth revealed ages ago to the prophets of Israel. This feeling is a vague feeling in the majority of cases. Few people could give a reasonable account of it. It is a something they have caught up from popular hearsay in a form they could scarcely define, and a something in which they place very little faith, but which at times of public peril like this, recurs to them with discomfort as a something in which there may be a foundation of truth somewhere if they could get at it. Educated people regard the whole matter as a popular delusion, and, therefore, beneath their attention. But even they, in times like these, have occasional qualms of apprehension that there may lurk some truth inside this popular tradition.

What is the foundation of this vague association of prophecy with the public events of these times ? On what does the tradition rest ? Is it possible to get an accurate and satisfactory knowledge of the subject ? Can it be shown, on the one hand, that it is possible rationally to trace the finger of God in these events, and to anticipate with clear reason, unusual and momentous issues from their culmination ? Or, on the other hand, can it be demonstrated that such a view is the mere fantasy of superstition ? An interesting enquiry, all will agree, at the present crisis, and one which it would be satisfactory to prosecute to one or other of these definite results.

The object of this pamphlet will be to show that the former of these hypotheses stands upon ground deserving the gravest consideration of all reasonable men. It will be a fact in favour of the attempt, that this is not the first time it has been made. The view to be advocated, as thousands of persons are aware, has been steadily and consistently presented for the last forty years, by the party represented by this pamphlet. A limited public have evidence of the truth of this statement in books, covering in the time occupied in their production, the period mentioned. Five vols. of the *Apostolic Advocate* (1836-40), edited by Dr. Thomas ; five vols. of the *Herald of the Future Age* (ditto) 1844-49 ; eleven vols. of the *Herald of the Kingdom and Age to Come* (ditto), 1850-61 ; twelve volumes of the *Christadelphian* (R. Roberts) 1861-76, (besides other works,—*Elpis Israel, Anatolia,*

Eureka, Twelve Lectures), constitute a mass of incontestible evidence
that the views presented in this pamphlet are not manufactured to suit
current facts. They are not like the conclusions of a man who, seeing
public events assume a certain shape, sets himself to work to construct
a theory to suit the circumstances; as in the case of the Baxterian
Louis Napoleon theory, which the writers of the foregoing literature
condemned long before its unfounded character was proclaimed to the
world by the catastrophe of Sedan, and the death of the inmate of
Chislehurst. They are rather the sober and reasonable anticipations
arising from a rational and reverential study of the prophetic word, at
a time when appearances were often against them, but which are
now being verified in a manner calculated to arrest the attention of all
who believe the Bible to be the word of God.

There is a general disposition, particularly among the educated, to
scout the application of prophecy to such subjects. The failure of
interpretation in the hands of fantastic and incompetent writers, is made
a reason for dismissing the whole subject from consideration or respect.
That this is reasonable will not be contended for by reasonable men.
It may be natural, but natural only with those who are influenced by
appearances. A subject that was not beneath the study and reverence
of the discoverer of gravitation, cannot lack claims on the attention
and confidence of the common run of men. Only those who reject the
Bible can consistently disregard the indications of the prophetic word;
and the Bible can not be rejected without doing violence to the
commonest elements of fact and evidence. This is not the place to
consider the claims of the Bible to our confidence. These remarks are
addressed to those who believe in the resurrection of Christ, and,
therefore, in the divinity of the Scriptures endorsed by him. Such
are aware that prophecy has been too signally fulfilled in the past to
leave any doubt as to its reliability for the future.

No man can be acquainted with the Bible without perceiving that
its prophecies are of a very exalted order. They are not the mere foretelling of events in the idle sense of telling beforehand what is going
to happen: they are the outlinings of the leading events in history
in so far only as they are related to the divine purpose on earth.
They do not include all histories or all the events of any history.
They are intended to throw light on God's purpose alone, and,
therefore, are found clustered around the one people on earth whom
He has chosen as the basis of His plan, in the past and future—the
Jews, of whom it is said " You only have I known of all the families
of the earth " (Amos. iii. 2); and again, " Salvation is of the Jews."—

(John iv. 22). The perception of this simple fact relieves the subject of many perplexities.

That in this channel, the events of the future have been foreshown is a demonstrable and important fact. The evidence is too extensive even to look at here. It will transpire in great measure in the course of the following pages. Meanwhile, it may not be without advantage to quote one or two express statements on the point: "Surely the Lord God will do nothing, but He revealeth His secret to His servants the prophets."—(Amos iii. 7.) "There is a God in heaven that revealeth secrets and maketh known to the king Nebuchadnezzar what shall come to pass in the latter days."—(Dan. ii. 28.) "The revelation of Jesus Christ which God gave unto him to shew unto His servants things which must shortly come to pass, and He sent and signified it by His angel unto His servant John."—(Rev. i. 1.) If these statements are true, we ought to be able to find recognizable and measurable light in the Scriptures on the leading events of history, and, therefore, on such a gigantic affair as the Eastern Question, which so radically affects and imperils great national interests, and involves the destiny of the land of Jehovah itself—now a pachalic of the threatened empire of Turkey.

But it may be objected that the affairs in question are perfectly human in their character. It may be said their origin can be so exactly traced to natural causes as to exclude the possible operation of occult influences. The Turks, it may be said, being a brutal race, have for centuries brutally treated the races that have been brought under their subjection by conquest, and that as a result, their empire is weak; and that Russia, by the operation of a perfectly natural ambition, desires possession of a desirable territory so evidently destined to fall out of Turkish hands by and bye: that, therefore, it is absurd to seek for a divine view of the case, or to regard the consequent events as forming any part of a divine programme.

The answer is obvious to those who accept the Bible and have made themselves familiar with its contents. We there discover that the springs of human action are accessible to divine control, and that men under the influence of· feelings perfectly natural to themselves are often made use of to accomplish things that God has purposed without their being in the least aware of it. Let two illustrations suffice where there are hundreds. Israel revolted from the law of God. In punishment for their revolt, God sent upon them the King of Assyria to desolate the land and subject the inhabitants to the horrors of invasion. The fact is stated thus: "O Assyrian, the rod of mine anger . . *I will send him* against a hypocritical nation, and against the people of my wrath *will I give him a charge."* At first sight, it would seem from this as if a direct and personal commission were sent by messenger to the Assyrian court, and that the Assyrian monarch acted in consequence as the witting and willing agent of Jehovah in the punishment of Israel. But this view is expressly excluded by what follows: we are given to understand that the Assyrian acted out his own view without even being aware that God was using him. It is added: "Howbeit, *he meaneth not so, neither doth his heart think so ;* but it is in his heart to destroy and to cut off nations not a few. For he saith, are not my princes altogether kings. . . He saith, By the strength of my hand I have done it. and by my wisdom, for I am prudent." The divine comment on the Assyrian pretensions in the case is unmistakable. It is this: "*Shall the axe boast itself against* HIM THAT HEWETH THEREWITH? *Or shall the saw magnify itself against* HIM THAT SHAKETH IT?"— (Isaiah x. 5, 13, 15.) Thus the Assyrian was aiming at the accomplishment of his own ambitions, in utter ignorance of the fact that God was using him as an axe to hew down the Israelitish tree of wickedness. The event was perfectly human in its character, so far as the agency was concerned, and yet was a divine operation intended to effectuate divine objects.

The other instance is similar: "Lo, *I raise up the Chaldeans,* that bitter and hasty nation, which shall march through the breadth of the land to possess the dwellings that are not theirs. . . He shall pass over and offend and impute this his power unto his God." What is the comment? "Lord, *Thou hast ordained them for judgment.* O mighty God, *Thou hast established them for correction."* —(Hab. i. 6, 12.) So also with the Roman invasion, foretold ages before by Moses as a divine visitation for the sins of Israel: the Romans were unconscious of being divinely guided in their proceedings. They but yielded to the natural impulse of conquest, and to those who witnessed their proceedings on the spot, there would have appeared to be nothing divine in the events.

On the same principle, the events now impending in the East may be of divine initiation and intent, though perfectly natural on the surface. The simple question is, Have these events been made the subject of prophecy? Have they any relation to the purpose of God on earth, as revealed to the prophets of Israel, and set forth in the writings in which they were instructed to record the revelation? If so, the perfect naturalness of them on the surface will be no bar to a divine construction of them by such as apprehend the facts involved in the foregoing argument.

The first clue is simple and palpable. It is a geographical one: *Turkey has possession of the Holy Land, and whatever happens to Turkey must affect that land as part of her dominion.* To see this fact in its true importance, we must look at another, viz., that *the Holy Land is the geographical basis of the Divine work upon earth.* No one will question this as regards the past. In the Holy Land the divine nation of Irrael was established. Moses and Joshua guided them thither from Egypt. In the Holy Land Samuel judged them, and David and Solomon reigned. In the Holy Land, Jesus, the Son of God, appeared, and lived his wondrous life, which in its effects has already largely changed the condition of mankind. The Bible is the book of the Holy Land. So much all admit concerning the past. But *is there no future for the Holy Land?*

This is the question which gives the Eastern embroglio its chiefest interest and importance. It is a question, the answer to which is one of the plainest things taught in the Bible, and yet to which there is the strongest opposition on the part of the great bulk of professing Christians. The answer is one which we must establish before we can hope to create for the Eastern Question that interest which sensible people, recognising the facts of the case, must feel; and before we can attract to it that amount of attention which it cannot fail to receive at the hands of such.

It is very easily established when once resurrection is accepted as the mode of future retribution; and the earth recognised as the arena of the divine purpose with regard to man living upon it.

The future portion of the righteous is frequently spoken of in the New Testament as "the inheritance," and this inheritance is said to be a thing promised.—(Gal. iii. 18.) Standing foremost—at the very beginning, indeed, of this promise—we find Abraham, in whose case we are able to localise the inheritance at the start. It is testified that Abraham had the honour to receive the promises— (Heb. xi. 17). "To Abraham and his seed were the promises made"—(Gal. iii. 16). As to the subject of the promise, so far as Abraham's personal part in it was concerned, we are informed that "God gave THE INHERITANCE to Abraham *by promise*"—(verse 18). Now what was this inheritance that was given to Abraham by promise? This question is answered by Paul in a way that is simple, conclusive, and in harmony with the meaning of the term and the facts of Abraham's case. "By faith Abraham, when he was called to go out into A PLACE *which he should after receive for* AN INHERITANCE, obeyed, and went out, not knowing whither he went. By faith he sojourned in *the land of promise* as in a strange country, dwelling in tabernacles with Isaac and Jacob, *the heirs with him* of the same promise."—(Heb. xi. 8, 9.) Here we have " a place" and " a land" as the subject of the promise of inheritance. There will, of course, be no question that this is the Holy Land, now in Turkish grasp, for it was in this Holy Land that Abraham, when he lived, sojourned as a stranger, and Isaac and Jacob after him.

The only question will be whether the promise was ever fulfilled. On this point, infidels take strong ground as against Christians of the popular type. They say Abraham never inherited the land, and that, therefore, the divine promise has failed. If it can be shown that Abraham is to receive possession of the land at the coming of Christ to set up the kingdom of his father David (Luke i. 32), the force of their argument is gone; but ordinary Christians do not believe this, and, consequently, have no answer to the infidel, except the unsatisfactory one that the promise was fulfilled in the occupation of the Holy Land by the Jews under the law of Moses.

But the answer indicated is the true one. The infidels, of course, are wrong; but so also are the Cristians when they deny that Abraham will receive the land for an inheritance, in which, in the days of his probation, he sojourned as a stranger. Their explanation that he received it when the Jewish nation occupied it under the law, is inconsistent with Paul's express reasoning on the subject. Paul says, " If the inheritance be of the law, it is no more of promise, but God gave it to Abraham *by promise.*"—(Gal. iii. 18.) He also says, " The promise that he should be the heir of the world *was* NOT *to Abraham or his seed through the law,* but through the righteousness of faith. " If they who are of the law be heirs, faith is made void, and the promise made of none effect."—(Rom. iv. 13.) Now the Jews held the land under the law of Moses, which made their occupation of it conditional on obedience to its provisions.—(See Deut. xxviii. entire). They did not render this obedience, and they were consequently scattered among the nations of the earth as at this day. *The dispersion of Israel is evidence that their occupation of the land of promise, was under the law and not under the promise.* Consequently, there remains a future occupation by Abraham under the promise; for it is beyond question that Abraham never inherited the land during his own life.—(Acts vii. 5; Gen. xxiii. 4; Heb. xi. 13).

It is this future occupation that forms the pivot of the entire prophetic scheme. Let anyone read the books of Isaiah, Jeremiah, Ezekiel, &c., &c., and he will be fully convinced of this. Two examples from the first of these books may suffice for what, without exaggeration, may be called hundreds. The second chapter foretells a day when "nation shall not lift up sword against nation, neither shall they learn war any more."—(Isaiah ii. 4.) There is no need to prove that this is future. Now, observe the geographical surroundings of this state of things. "The *mountain of the house of the Lord* shall be exalted above the hills. . . . . The law shall go forth *from Zion :* and the word of the Lord *from Jerusalem*"—(verses 2, 3). The 25th chapter foretells (verse 8) a day when tears will be wiped from all faces, and death shall be swallowed up of victory. There is no need to prove that this is yet future. Observe, then, the geographical surroundings identical with the other case. " In that day shall this song be sung in *the land of Judah*"—(xxvi. 1). " The Lord of Hosts shall reign *in Mount Zion and in Jerusalem*"—(xxiv. 23). The whole of the prophets have the same characteristic : *their delineations of the coming glory are interwoven inseparably with the land promised to Abraham.*

Let not the reader regard this as an unimportant fact. Let him not suppose it is unconnected with the glory and the work of Christ. Let him remember that the spirit of Christ in the prophets " testified beforehand the sufferings of Christ and THE GLORY THAT SHOULD FOLLOW " (1 Peter i. 11), and that therefore the writings of the prophets, which Peter styles " the sure word of prophecy," is " a light in a dark place, *until the day dawn,*" to which " we do well that we take heed "—(2 Peter i. 19). The day spoken of has not yet dawned, but it will arise in due time, and that due time there is reason to believe to be near at hand, as will appear in what is to follow. It is the day of the glory of the Holy Land, as the inheritance of the chosen of God, and the scene of the exaltation of Jesus, returned in power and great glory, to sit on the throne of David, and reign over all peoples, nations and languages.—(Isaiah ix. 6; Jer. xxiii. 5; Luke i. 32; Dan. vii. 15; Rev. xi. 15).

CHAPTER II.

The reason for looking for the end in our day—Expiration of the prophetic periods—Widespread expectation of Christ's appearing as at his first advent—Approaching revival of Jewish prosperity—Consequent necessity for Turkish dissolution—The symbolic representation of these things in the Apocalypse.

HAVING answered the question, *Is there no future to the Holy Land?* the next point to consider is, the reason for looking at this particular time in the world's history for events of special significance as bearing on the Holy Land. Why, in the nineteenth century, any more than in the fifth, or tenth, or fifteen, or thirtieth, should we look for the occurrence of events tending to precipitate the destiny of the land of promise, and to introduce the great day of glory so long foreshadowed in the sure word of prophecy?

The answer to this question is susceptible of very extensive treatment. We must be content with a mere indication of it. In brief it is this, that in our day the period expires which has been appointed for the desolation of Israel and their land, in punishment for their sins. There are several illustrations of this. The period of Gentile supremacy has been measured and defined in various ways in the prophetic word, and the working out of all the specifications—checking and counterchecking one another—leads to the same result. One illustration of how the result is arrived at must suffice.

It is well to remember that at the first advent of Christ, just before his appearance, there was a widespread expectation, both in the Jewish and Pagan worlds, that this appearance would take place, though no definite idea existed as to its manner and effect. The fact of this expectation is testified to both by Josephus and Tacitus, both writers of the first century. The reason of the expectation was that a prophecy had been recorded by Daniel (chapter ix. 24-26), that in seventy weeks (of years) from the date of the Persian decree for the rebuilding of Jerusalem, after her seventy years' desolation at the hands of Babylon, the Messiah should appear. This period was about to expire at the time Jesus appeared; hence the widespread expectation and the saying of Jesus: "The time is fulfilled: the kingdom of God is at hand; repent ye, and believe the gospel."—(Mark i. 15.) In our day, there is again a widespread expectation of his appearance, and the reason is of the same sort. Certain periods prophetically specified as those at the end of which he will re-appear, expire in our generation.

Jesus, foretelling the everthrow of the Jewish state, said, "Jerusalem shall be trodden down of the Gentiles *until the times of the Gentiles be fulfilled."* — (Luke xxi. 25). When did these "times of the Gentiles" begin? and how long do they last? If we can ascertain these two points, we know the conclusion of the times. There is a prophecy on this subject in Daniel viii., on which it is necessary to remark that it is a symbolic prophecy in which events of magnitude are represented by petty objects, and time is also signified on a reduced scale; but, at the same time, accompanied by explanations that make it plain. The time is measured on the scale of a day for a year, as expressed by Ezek. iv. 5: "I have appointed thee each day for a year;" and conclusively illustrated by the crucifixion, which it was foretold (Dan. ix. 24-26) would occur at the end of seventy weeks from the Persian edict for the rescue of Jerusalem from her Babylonish desolation. Seventy weeks are 490 days, and the period from B.C. 456 (the date of the edict by the hand of Nehemiah in the twentieth year of the reign of Artaxerxes.—Nehemiah ii. 1-8) to the crucifixion, was 490 years.

In the prophecy to which I refer (Dan. viii.), Daniel was shown a ram, a goat, horns, stars, and an army, with the Holy Land as the base of the symbol. He observed certain movements among the objects of the symbol, and received certain explanations by which we are enabled to read the meaning of them. The explanation, in brief, was (verses 20-24) that the ram and goat with horns represented the Persian, Greek and Roman powers in their hostile relation to the land and people of the Jews. The holy nation was to be prevailed against by these powers successively. This foreshadowing has been verified in history as our own eyes witness, for the Jews and their land are yet unrecovered from the great Roman catastrophe.

The principal point is the question of time. Daniel heard one personage in the vision ask another how long a period of time the vision would cover—(verse 13.) The answer was (verse 14), "Until *two thousand three hundred days:* then shall the sanctuary be cleansed." There is an alternative reading of this number. The Septuagint and certain ancient Hebrew MSS., have "two thousand *four* hundred." This difference, however, is deprived of its embarrassment by the fact that 2,400 years have elapsed since the commencement of the events of the vision, shewing the 2,300 reading to be the incorrect one. Now, the first event seen in the vision was the uprise of the two-horned ram. The ram was explained to mean the double-dynastied power of Persia. Consequently, if we get the date of the establishment of the empire of Darius and Cyrus, we get the commencement of the 2,400 year-days, and a clue to our present whereabouts with regard to the end of it. History points to about B.C. 540 as the date in question. This figure, added to the present year 1877, gives 2,417 as the number of years that have elapsed since the commencement of the events symbolised in the vision. It is that number of years since the political ram appeared in the arena of imperial power. In a word, the time for Israel's desolation is past, and we are in the era of the revival signified by the words "then shall the sanctuary be cleansed," or, in other words, the resuscitation of the Jewish power, which is predicted by other prophets in very plain terms. This furnishes the true meaning of the many events that are now tending to bring the Jewish nation and the Jewish land into prominence; and is one of the several facts which justify the believing reader of the Word of God, in regarding this particular century with special interest and anticipation, in connection with the predicted return of favour to Zion.

The approach of favour to Zion must involve the dissolution of the power that acts the part of her desolator as that time approaches. In this light alone, the decay of the Turkish empire and her threatened disappearance from the scene altogether, is an interesting and significant fact.

But without something in the nature of more special indication on the subject, we should be unable to attach that amount of interest to the Eastern Question which scripturally belongs to it. This more special indication we find in another part of the word of God, and to that we must now look. It is a part of God's word, against which a great amount of prejudice exists, even on the part of such as regard it as divine. It is the last book in the Bible. The prejudice against it is without true reason, and can only be entertained by such as are not practically acquainted with it.

What is the nature of this book? It is defined in its very first sentence: "The revelation of Jesus Christ which God gave unto him to show unto His servants THINGS WHICH MUST SHORTLY COME TO PASS."—(Rev. i. 1.) A concluding statement of the book confirms this representation of its character: "I, Jesus, have sent mine angel to testify unto you these things in the churches."—(Rev. xxii. 16.) The book is, therefore, a message from Christ, setting forth certain things that were about to happen among men, that his servants might know beforehand, and be prepared to estimate public events in their divine light, and to frame their action accordingly. No man receiving Revelations as divine can deny this.

From this it follows that the message is capable of being understood; for how otherwise could it " show unto his servants " the things represented ? The message is communicated in symbol and enigma, it is true; but it is accompanied with words of explanation here and there, which act as keys to the diligent and the wise, and by them it may be unlocked. Knowledge concealed but not absolutely inaccessible is more interesting than what is spread on the surface; and, in this case, there was a special reason for concealing it: that it might be withheld from the undeserving class, who were to be the agents in transacting the events foretold. Its intelligibility to those who set themselves to understand, is manifest from the occurrence of such statements as this : " *Here is the mind that hath wisdom :* the seven heads are seven mountains on which the woman sitteth," &c.

Now, when Revelations is thoroughly dissected (see *Eureka :* Dr. Thomas's Exposition of the Apocalypse), it is found to set forth, symbolically, yet in chronological order, the leading features of European history during the interval lying between the day when it was given to John in Patmos and the time when Christ should reappear, and when " The kingdoms of this world should become the kingdoms of our Lord and His Christ, and he should reign for ever and ever."—(Rev. xi. 15.) The framework of the scheme by which all these events are exhibited is on the basis of the number seven— the numerical symbol of completeness. Opening with messages to seven particular churches, as representing all the rest, there is introduced a book or scroll, sealed with seven seals, after the ancient custom—the closed book representing unknown futurity, and the seals its subdivisions of time. The first seal is broken, and certain things are exhibited appertaining to the first historical period coming after A.D. 98—the time when the revelation was given; then the second seal is broken, and the events of the next succeeding period exhibited ; then the third seal is broken, and so on to the seventh. The events of the seventh seal comprise a new subdivision of the time succeeding to it: seven angels are introduced with trumpets. A trumpet is an instrument to summon soldiers or servants, and the trumpets are used here to symbolise the judgments which God should bring on Europe for the corruption of His way. The judgments historically come one after the other in the order of the trumpets. The first angel sounds, and certain symbolic occurrences ensue, representing the events that transpired during the period symbolised. Then the second angel sounds, and certain other things take place which correspond to the events of the period next ensuing, and so on to the seventh. Then a new symbol is introduced for the subdivision of the remaining time. Among the events of the seventh trumpet, seven angels receive seven vials, which they empty one after another on certain specified objects and areas, with consumptive effects, after the analogy of chemical transformations. In most cases, they waste away the things that were brought upon the scene in judgment by the trumpets.

The entire representation covers the period lying between the prosperous days of the Roman Empire under Hadrian and the Antonines, to the catastrophe of Russo-headed militarism at Armageddon, ensuing upon the disappearance of the Turkish empire under the sixth vial. It is under the sixth vial that we meet with the Eastern question, so far as the Apocalypse is concerned. The sixth trumpet brings the Turks into Europe under the symbol of fiery horsemen (see Rev. ix. 13-21); the sixth vial dries up their power under the symbol of the river Euphrates. That this is the meaning of the symbol, is evident from the fact: first, that waters in oceanic collection are employed to represent the populations of the world. Thus, " the waters that thou sawest are peoples, and multitudes, and nations, and tongues" (Rev. xvii. 15); and second, that a local water, such as a river, is employed to represent the power in occupation of the territory irrigated by it. Thus the aggressive power of Assyria is spoken of under the symbol of its principal river in a state of inundation: " The Lord shall bring upon thee (Israel) the waters of the river, strong and many, even the king of Assyria, and all his glory ; and he shall come up over all his channels and overflow all his banks." —(Isaiah viii. 7, 8.) This is a political figure, of which there are other illustrations. For the sixth angel to pour his vial upon the river Euphrates, therefore, is to intimate the adverse operation of Providence against the power of whose territory the Euphrates is the characteristic river, viz., the Turkish power, of which the symbol is the more appropriate, in that the Turkish power, geographically speaking, is of Euphratean origin in relation to Europe. The object of this adverse operation is clearly stated : " And the sixth angel poured out his vial upon the great river Euphrates ; and *the water thereof was dried up*, that the way of the kings of the East might be prepared."— (Rev. xvi. 12.) What is this but the gradual exhaustion of the Ottoman power? This was seen to be the meaning two hundred years ago by Tillinghast, who remarked upon the improbability of the prophecy from a human point of view, as at that time the Turkish power was the strongest upon earth. A writer also at the beginning of the present century remarked to the same effect, expressing his inability to imagine by what means so great a power as the Ottoman power then was could be brought to a state of decay. In our day, the decayed state of the Ottoman power is the most notorious fact of European politics, and its downfall has been a matter of expectation throughout the world for a considerable time. This fact is one of the great signs of the times from a Bible point of view. It indicates the proximity of the events to which the sixth vial stands related. The nature of these we shall presently see. Suffice it here to say that they comprise the Russian conquest of Turkey, the re-organization of the Jewish nationality on a limited scale, war between England and Russia, and the re-appearance of Christ upon earth, to change the face of the scene.

CHAPTER III.

Daniel's " time of the end "—Its nature defined—Its coincidence with Ezekiel's " latter days "—The sixth vial's relation to that now-current period of the world's history—The object of Turkey's decay from a providential point of view—The imminent uprise of a new order of Kings.

In the book of the prophet Daniel we read of " the time of the end." —(Dan. xi. 40.) The nature of the " end " involved in this phrase is defined as " the end *of the days.*"—(Dan. xii. 13.) The " days," so far as the one period which we have looked at is concerned, begin with the domination of the Persian Empire over the Holy Land. They number 2,400. It is that number of years and a little more since Cyrus reigned. Consequently, the prophetic " days " which represent years, are ended, and our generation marks " the time of their end." This conclusion is yielded by several other periods, for the exhibition of which in detail we must refer to works advertised herewith. That which in Daniel is spoken of as " the time of the end," is in Ezekiel described as " the latter days " and " the latter years."—(Ezekiel xxxviii. 8, 16).

The sixth vial is a symbolic representation of the events that belong to this "time of the end"—this overlapping margin styled "the latter days." This is evident, not only from the position in which the sixth vial is found when the events of the Apocalypse, as a whole, are chronologically traced, but from the coincidence of its terminal events with those of Daniel's "time of the end" and Ezekiel's "latter days." It is this fact which invests the sixth vial with such especial interest as furnishing a clue for the reading of current public events in their bearing upon the divine programme which is being worked out in the affairs of men, and which ultimates in the overthrow of all human power, and the establishment of a divine universal despotism in the hands of Jesus, enthroned in Zion.

Its bearing on the state of Turkey we have seen, but we have not considered the statement as to the object divinely purposed in the removal of Turkey: "that the way of the kings of the east might be prepared." This statement will be comprehended by those who apprehend the argument of the chapter bearing on the Holy Land. The great event that is looming, is the re-establishment of Jehovah's kingdom in the land of promise, in the hands of a new order of kings. These kings are the saints (1 Cor. vi. 2; Dan. vii. 27); a mighty company, who are απο ανατολων ηλιου—translated "from the east," but more exactly, "from the risings of the sun." They spring into being at the rising of the Sun of Righteousness (Mal. iv. 2), viz., at the return of the Lord Jesus, who says, in connection with this very sixth vial: "Behold, *I come as a thief*; blessed is he that watcheth." These saints—comprehensive of "the dead . . . . . Thy servants, the prophets, and the saints, and they who fear Jehovah's name, small and great" (Rev. xi. 18)—are styled the "seed of Abraham, *and heirs according to the promise.*"—(Gal. iii. 29.) Consequently, they are the coming inheritors with Abraham of the land in which he sojourned as a stranger. When they inherit it, they inherit it in power and great glory, as the lords of mankind—the rulers of the new order of things, when "The Lord shall be king over all the earth," and the saints shall reign kings and priests with him.—(Zech. xiv. 9; Rev. v. 10; xx. 5.)

Now as a preparation for the events that develop this new order of things, the Turkish power, which obstructs "the way" by its desolating presence in the Holy Land, has to be removed. With this view, it has been gradually drying up, through a series of providentially-regulated circumstances; and at this moment stands on the verge of destruction. If we had no other light than is contained in the symbolography of the sixth vial, we should not know whether Turkey would continue to the end, or be overthrown by another power. But we have other light, and know that she is destined to fall in her decrepitude in the arms of Russia.

* * *

CHAPTER IV.

The frog section of the sixth vial—The effects of French diplomacy—Gigantic armaments of the present hour—Despairing prospect apart from prophecy—War preparations an appointed condition of the end—" The war of the great day of God Almighty "—Its object the punishment and purification of the world.

THERE is another matter in the sixth vial which is very important to understand. While the Euphrates was drying, John saw (Rev. xvi. 13) three frog-shaped things emerge from the mouths of three great symbols, the dragon, the beast and false prophet, representing three great systems in Europe. The spirits like frogs went forth from these centres to the nations of the earth, with this mission : " *to gather them to the war* (for the word in the original is πολεμος) *of that great day of God Almighty.*"—(verse 14.)

We shall not devote much space to the consideration of the frogs, as it is the result of their mission that is more particularly to be regarded. Suffice it to say that they must represent influences at work while the political Euphrates is drying, for they form part and parcel of the same vial ; second, they must be political influences, for only political influences gather nations to war ; and third, they must be identified with a power associated in political heraldry with the frog, as the rule of symbolic prophecy is to adopt the symbols used by nations to represent their power : *e.g.*, the winged lion of Babylon, the ram of Persia, the goat of Greece, &c. These principles of elucidation point to France, which commenced its national career under the symbol of a frog, on banner, shield and coin, representative of the marshy country of Westphalia in which the Franks had their origin ; which has, till the downfall of the French empire, been a potent intriguing influence in European affairs, concurrently with the decay of the Ottoman empire ; and which, during the reign of Napoleon III. diplomatically went forth with war-causing effects, from 1. Constantinople (the mouth of the Pagan dragon of apocalyptic symbolism) leading to the Crimean war; 2. Vienna (the mouth of the earth-beast of Rev. xiii. 11 : leading to the Austro-Sardinian war; 3. Rome (the mouth of the false prophet of European ecclesiasticism), causing the Garibaldo-Italian war. The combined result of these diplomatic and military frog-excited disturbances of the European system, is to be seen in the gigantic armaments of the present hour. By universal conscription and other means, indirectly stimulated into development by French political influence, the world is now prepared for war as it never has been in any period of the world's history. Beforetime, nations *had* armies: now they are armies. Every man in Europe is a soldier, on or off duty. What does it mean? No man knows apart from prophecy. Well-wishers of their kind stand aghast at the spectacle presented by civilised Europe as one vast camp. Away from the light shed by prophecy, we might well despair.

But prophecy sheds great light on the subject. The symbolism of the sixth vial shows us that unprecedented war preparation was appointed for the time of the end, and was to be providentially developed by the political Franco-frogs of the nineteenth century. It shows us also what it is leading up to: it is a preparation for the great appointed collision between God and man, when the world is to be punished, and prepared for the righteous government of Christ by a time of unparalleled judgment. Such a crisis was foretold by other prophets long before the days of John. John's revelation is in fact an exhibiton, in greater detail than had been before revealed, of the things foreshown to the prophets of former ages. (Any one may satisfy himself of the identity of John's revelation and previous prophecy, by consulting the following passages in Revelations: chap. x. 7; xix. 10; xxii. 6, 9.)

In what was shown to the prophets before the days of John, nothing is more clearly revealed than that the time of the end would be a time of general war-preparation, and at last of general war, in which the power of man should be universally broken by divine judgments in the transition from the kingdom of man to the kingdom of God. A few illustrations of this may be in place. In Joel we read (and that what we read appertains to the latter-day restoration of Israel, will be apparent to even a superficial reader of the context):—

" Proclaim ye this among the Gentiles ; prepare war, wake up the mighty men ; let all the men of war draw near ; let them come up. Beat your plowshares into swords and your pruning-hooks into spears ; let the weak say I am strong. Assemble yourselves and come, all ye heathen, and gather yourselves together round about ; and (*marginal reading*) the Lord shall bring down His mighty ones."

In Zech. xiv. 2-4, 9, we read thus :

" I will gather all nations against Jerusalem to battle. . . . Then shall the Lord go forth and fight against those nations as when He fought in the day of battle. And His feet shall stand on that day upon the Mount of Olives, which is before Jerusalem on the east. . . . And the Lord shall be king over all the earth ; in that day, there shall be one Lord and His name one."

Zeph. iii. 8, speaks in the same strain :

" My determination is to gather the nations that I may assemble the kingdoms to pour upon them mine indignation, even all my fierce anger ; for all the earth shall be devoured with the fire of my jealousy."

Isaiah, by the Spirit, pictures the situation as follows, xvii. 12-14 :

" Woe to the multitude of many people, which make a noise like the noise of the seas ; and to the rushing of nations that make a rushing like the rushing of mighty waters. The nations shall rush like the rushing of many waters, but God shall rebuke them, and they shall flee afar off, and shall be chased like the chaff of the mountains before the wind and like thistle-down before the whirlwind. And behold at eveningtide trouble, and before the morning, he is not. This is the portion of them that trouble us and the lot of them that rob us."

Other illustrations are as follow :

" Enter into the rock and hide thee in the dust, for fear of the Lord and for the glory of His Majesty. The lofty looks of man shall be humbled and the haughtiness of men shall be bowed down, and the Lord alone shall be exalted in that day. . . . They shall go into the holes of the rocks and into the caves of the earth, for fear of the Lord and for the glory of His Majesty, when He ariseth to shake terribly the earth."—(Is. ii. 10, 11, 19.)

" He (Jehovah) shall judge among many people, and *rebuke strong nations afar off*, and they shall beat their swords into plowshares and their spears into pruning hooks."—(Micah iv. 3.)

" I will give thee (the Son) the heathen for thy inheritance, and the uttermost parts of the earth for thy possession. And thou shalt break them with a rod of iron, and dash them in pieces like a potter's vessel."—(Ps. ii. 8.)

" And I saw the Beast and the kings of the earth and their armies gather together, to make war against him that sat on the horse and against his army " (Rev. xix. 19). " These (ten kings) shall make war with the Lamb, and the Lamb shall overcome them."—(Rev. xvii. 14.)

These citations from the prophetic testimony amply confirm the statement that the time of the end is a time of war, and that its closing episode could not be more appropriately designated than by the Apocalyptic phrase : " THE WAR OF THE GREAT DAY OF GOD ALMIGHTY." The period, as a whole, is styled " The day of the Lord's vengeance."—(Isaiah lxiii. 4 ; xxxiv. 8.) Christ's work at the crisis is said to be that of treading the winepress of Jehovah's anger (Rev. xix. 15; Joel iii. 13); taking vengeance on them that know not God and obey not the gospel of our Lord Jesus Christ. (2 Thess. i. 8.) By Daniel, it is described as " a time of trouble such as never was since there was a nation upon earth " (Dan. xii. 1); and he goes on to state that the incidents of the situation include the resurrection of some to everlasting life and some to shame and everlasting contempt. The general character of the period is graphically pourtrayed in the following quotation from Jeremiah :

" For, lo, I begin to bring evil on the city which is called by my name, and should ye be utterly unpunished ? Ye shall not be unpunished ; For I will call for a sword upon all the inhabitants of the earth, saith the Lord of hosts. Therefore prophesy thou against them all these words, and say unto them, the Lord shall roar from on high and utter His voice from His holy habitation ; He shall mightily roar upon His habitation ; He shall give a shout as they that tread the grapes against all the inhabitants of the earth. A noise shall come even to the ends of the earth ; for the Lord hath a controversy with the nations: He will plead with all flesh ; He will give them that are wicked to the sword, saith the Lord. Thus saith the Lord of hosts, Behold evil shall go forth from nation to nation, and a great whirlwind shall be raised up from the coasts of the earth. And the slain of the Lord shall be at that day from one end of the earth even unto the other end of the earth ; they shall not be lamented, neither gathered, nor buried ; they shall be dung upon the ground."

The effect of this period of tempest, at first sight calculated to be destructive of the human species, is defined in the following language : " When thy judgments are in the earth, *then will the inhabitants of the world learn righteousness.*"—(Isaiah xxvi. 9.) " *All nations shall come and worship before* thee, for thy judgments are made manifest " (Rev. xv. 4). " Come, and behold the works of the Lord, what desolations He hath made. He maketh war to cease unto the ends of the earth. . . . Be still and know that I am God. *I will be exalted among the heathen : I will be exalted in the earth.* . . . All nations whom Thou hast made *shall come and worship before Thee, O Lord, and shall glorify Thy name,* for Thou art great and doest wondrous things " (Psa. xlvi. 8-10 ; lxxxvi. 9).

CHAPTER V.

The particular shape of the conflict—The predictions of Daniel and Ezekiel —The war between Turkey and Egypt thirty years ago—Identification of Russia as the subject of prophecy—Her destined overthrow of Turkey sooner or later—The situation preparing before our eyes.

FROM all this, it will be seen that the symbolism of the sixth vial is only in harmony with the rest of the Scriptures in representing a war-like attitude, and finally a war-making policy on the part of all the nations of the world as the characteristic of the time of the end. The particular shape of the conflict as it approaches its last dread crisis, when the judgments of God—ministered by Christ, personally returned to the earth—become a visible element of the situation, is also revealed ; and it is the revelation on this point (next to the decay of the Turkish empire) that imparts to the Eastern Question its peculiar interest from a scriptural point of view.

This revelation is contained in two notable prophecies—one by Daniel and the other by Ezekiel. That of Daniel first merits attention. It is in the 11th chapter of his book. The chapter has to do with two kings who are called, with reference to their geographical relation to Jerusalem (as will be apparent to the intelligent reader), " the king of the north " and " the king of the south." The prophetic sketch comprises the period extending from the days of the Persian Xerxes to " the time of the end," which is introduced in verse 40. After the overthrow of the Persian monarchy by Alexander the Great, the Greek empire, on Alexander's death, was divided into four independent sections, which may be roughly specified as Macedonia, Persia, Syria, and Egypt. The two last were north and south of Jerusalem, and their kings are spoken of as " the king of the south " and " the king of the north " throughout the chapter, with the modifications imposed by the changes of history. The history of their wars is prophetically given with considerable minuteness down to a certain point. Then Rome appears on the territory of the king of the north, and we have the history of the intervening ages compressed into two or three verses (36-39), and then " the time of the end " is introduced at verse 40. This time we have reached, as before indicated, and in our day the Sultan of Turkey occupies the territory anciently occupied by " the king of the north " of the principal part of the chapter ; and the quasi-independent Viceroy of Egypt, the territory of the king of the south. There is therefore no difficulty in placing the prophecy in its modern applications in those two cases.

But there is a second king of the north introduced at the time of the end—a king north of the northern king of Dan. xi. This is manifest from the description of what is to happen at the time of the end. Thus: "at the time of the end, the king of the south shall push at him (the king of the north); and the king of the north shall come against him (the king of the north"). Thus, the power which is spoken of throughout the chapter as "the king of the north," is at the time of the end itself assailed by a power farther north than itself, and therefore by a power which at the time of the end, is emphatically "the king of the north." In the days of the Ptolemies and the Antiochuses, there was no such power. The earth to the north of them was an unsubdued waste of barbarians, without nationality or cohesion. But in our day—in "the time of the end"—the situation is entirely changed. To the north of the northernmost section of the divided empire of the Greeks, is a colossal power of ever-growing extent and solidity. In "the autocrat of the north,"—for his dominion girdles the northern zone in Europe and Asia,—we have a power exactly answering to the implications of the prophecy as it approaches "the time of the end." The position of the Sultan, as lord of both the Macedonian and Syrian sections of the divided empire of the ancient Greeks, leaves no doubt as to his being the subject of this time-of-the-end prophecy. We have but to look at his political surroundings, to be able to see its drift with regard to his future. The prophecy is—

"At the time of the end shall the king of the south push at him, and the king of the north shall come against him like a whirlwind, with chariots and with horsemen, and with many ships, and he shall enter into the countries and shall overflow and pass over. He shall enter also into the glorious land, and many countries shall be overthrown. . . . The land of Egypt shall not escape."—(Dan. xi. 40-42.)

First, we have the king of the south introduced to notice in his latter-day relation to the occupier of Macedon and Syria, which is Turkey. We look at Egypt and enquire if modern history supplies the required parallel. Egypt, it is true, is nominally part of the Turkish empire; but she is a practically independent power for all that. She has her own government and her own king. She pays a tribute to Constantinople, but makes her own wars, and enacts her own laws, without any power on the part of the Sultan to interfere.

Has Egypt "pushed at" the Sultan in this "time of the end?" The elder living generation is witness to the answer. Not long before the terrible revolutions of 1848, Mehemet Ali, the ruler of Egypt, made war on the Sultan, and carried his invasion of Turkey successfully as far as Smyrna, and would to all appearances have overthrown the Sultan's power altogether if the " Great Powers " had not interfered, and by force compelled Mehemet Ali to evacuate Syria, surrender the Turkish fleet, which had revolted to him ; and retire to Egypt with a recognition of the right of his lineal successors to the throne of the country. The " *king of the south pushed at* " the Syro-Macedonian " king of the north :" having " pushed," he had to retire ; but not so with the next enemy of the pushed-at power. This enemy,—situated to the north of the Syro-Macedonian king of the north,—" comes against him like a whirlwind," and overthrows the many countries in his possession.

That this northern time-of-the-end vanquisher of the latter-day occupant of Syria and Macedonia (Turkey) is Russia, is made certain by Ezekiel's portraiture of him. The description will be found in chapters 38 and 39 of the prophet, and is well worth attentive perusal by those who earnestly desire to know the truth of the matter. We have already remarked on the time to which the prophecy relates. It is specified in verse 16, chapter xxxviii: " It shall be *in the latter days.*" The power described is exhibited in the light of an invader of Syria (now in Turkish possession): " In the latter years, thou shalt come unto the land that is brought back from the sword and is gathered out of many people, *against the mountains of Israel which have been always waste,* but it is brought forth out of the nations, and they shall dwell safely all of them. Thou shalt ascend and come like a storm ; thou shalt be like a cloud to cover the land, thou and all thy bands and many people with thee " (verses 8 and 9). Who is this that is thus addressed, and to whom is assigned this latter-day invasion of territories now forming part of the Turco-northern horn of Daniel's Greek goat? The answer is found in the opening verses of the chapter, particularly verse 2 : " Prince of Rosh, Mesheck and Tubal." The English version does not give " Rosh :" the Greek (Septuagint) version does. Why the difference? Simply because Rosh is both a proper name and a general term, and it is a matter of judgment which is to be chosen. As a general term, Rosh means chief ; as a proper name it points to the region where according to Gesenius, the Roschi lived, whose name survives in modern geographical nomenclature in the form of

Russia and Russians. Which does it mean in the prophecy? Its association with other geographical terms would indicate the latter. The Seventy were of this opinion, and certainly their judgment is of more weight, living over 2,000 years ago, and possessing a better knowledge of the ancient names of countries than English translators only 300 years ago. But the identification of Russia with the power spoken of is not dependent upon the term Rosh. It comes out of the other terms—Meshech and Tubal, which have their modern and modified equivalents in Moscovy and Tobolsk. "The land of Magog" points to Germany, and indicates a Russo-German combination in the operations described. The identification of Russia is completed by the statement in verse 15: "Thou shalt come out of *thy place in the north parts.*"

Russia is to be leader in an extensive confederacy. This is evident from the following language:—" I will bring thee forth and all thine army . . . Persia, Ethiopia and Lybia with them, all of them with shield and helmet. Gomer and all his bands, the house of. Togarmah of the north quarters and all his bands, and many people with thee. Be thou prepared and prepare for thyself, thou and all thy company that are assembled unto thee, and be thou a guard unto them. . . . I will bring thee against my land."—(Verses 1-7; 16.) This presents us with the specific form of that military gathering of nations described generally in the passages quoted earlier in the pamphlet.

We see the situation in preparation before our eyes. For years Russia has been steadily advancing towards the position of European leadership. Her territorial expansion has at the same time progressed at a rate exceeding all other countries put together, and in a way (particularly in Asia) to cause great concern to a certain class of politicians who fear Russian aggression on India. The celebrated will of Peter the Great, whether genuine or spurious, has been faithfully followed, and Russia is steadily advancing to a position which promises the acquisition of universal dominion. At the present moment she has succeeded in allying all Europe diplomatically with herself against Turkey; and her armies are massing in Bessarabia, under a very distinct intimation from the Czar that he intends to extort by arms what Turkey has refused to the assembled Ambassadors of Europe. In such a case, we all know that the exactions of the sword go far beyond the requests of diplomacy. War between Russia and Turkey must be. It is precisely the event required by the times, and its result, whether immediately or subsequently, will lay Turkey in the dust, and plant Russia both in Constantinople and Egypt. There may be a little tortuosity and length in the road, but it has only one ending, and that ending may be reached without delay. The advanced state of the times and the language of the prophecy seem alike to require celerity in the triumph of the arms of the north. Turkey down, there may be a lull for the development of the final combination which brings Russia and England to a death-struggle on the mountains of Israel, the exigencies and momentous results of which will engage our consideration in another chapter.

CHAPTER VI.

Britain's part in the coming conflict—The parties to the struggle—Its beginning—Its clouds and portents now overhanging the world—The part that belongs to the Jews—At first an unarmed agricultural colony in Palestine—The Jews defended from Russian aggression by Tarshish—The evidence that modern Britain is ancient Tarshish.—A difficulty met.

BRITAIN'S part in the coming conflict is involved, though not expressed, in the symbolography of Rev. xvi. It is comprehended in the phrase which we have already had to look at : "the war of the great day of God Almighty." The events of the sixth vial period have to do with preparing the situation for that war. The first event—the decay and removal of the Turkish Empire—clears the country where it is to take place, viz., the Holy Land, as revealed by Joel, Ezekiel, and the other prophets already quoted. The second event—the operation and results of the Franco-political intrigues symbolised by the frogs—develops such a situation among the nations of the earth, as that they shall be ready to participate in such a mighty struggle. Both these things are far advanced in their accomplishment. The appointed sequel becomes now the natural object of expectancy.

The parties to the struggle, in its preliminary form are four in number. They are, as we have seen, 1, Russia ; 2, the Jews ; 3, a power friendly to the Jews (to which as yet only allusion has been made) ; and 4, the Almighty, in the person of His glorified Son, returned to earth a second time, to break in pieces the governments of men, and establish himself on the throne of David as universal king.—(Acts i. 11; iii. 20; Psalm ii. 8; Luke i. 32; Isaiah ix. 6; Jer. xxiii. 5; Dan. vii. 15.) The prophecies already quoted show that war is in actual progress among the three first, when the divine element supervenes. "The war of the great day of God Almighty" begins in the diplomatic and military sphere, and is, in its first stages, to all appearance, perfectly natural. Its clouds and portents are now overhanging the world. Russia wanted to avert the Eastern Question, which all European statesmen regard with dread. England was still more strongly of the same mind; but the hands of both have been forced by the action of Slavonic societies and the barbarities of the Turks. The question which they were labouring to keep dormant, has burst in terrific blaze before the world. That which they feared to allude to in their private despatches, has become the subject of open and peremptory discussion at a public Conference of the assembled Powers of Europe—a Conference which England a year ago emphatically refused; which she now takes the leading part in, and at which she is in agreement with Russia against Turkey in opposition to the cherished policy of forty years. And the Conference assembled to make peace, has only made war more certain for Europe and more fatal to the doomed Ottoman.

We have already looked at the part prophetically assigned to Russia: it is to overthrow Turkey in conjunction with other powers with which she is confederated as the leader and head. The part that belongs to the Jews is at first a subordinate one. In the estimation of politicians, the Jews will be an absolutely insignificant element in the situation. Yet they are the kernel of the whole question from a divine point of view, as the sequel will prove; that is, the Jewish nationality, in a new form, will be the pivot around which all the subsequent evolutions will develop themselves; and the centre in which all political power will be absorbed, and from which a new and unparalled conquest will be effected, resulting in the submission of all nations to the sceptre of the house of David, in the hands of the Son of David returned to reign where he was crucified.

In the beginning of the struggle, the Jews are a feeble and newly-formed colony in the previously long desolate land of Israel. Anyone may be convinced of this by reading Ezekiel's description of their state at the time of the Russian invasion. The description has already been quoted in part, but it was for another purpose, and may be reproduced without detriment :—

" In the latter years, thou shalt come into the land that is brought back from the sword, and *is gathered out of many people;* against the mountains of ̄Israel, *which have been always waste,* BUT IT IS BROUGHT FORTH OUT OF THE NATIONS, and they shall dwell safely all of them. Thou shalt ascend and come like a storm. Thou shalt be like a cloud to cover the land, thou and all thy bands, and many people with thee. . . . Thou shalt think an evil thought, and thou shalt say, " I will go up to *the land of unwalled villages.* I will go to them that are *at rest*—that dwell safely all of them, *dwelling without walls and having neither bars nor gates,* to take a spoil and take a prey ; to turn thine hand upon the *desolate places that are now inhabited,* and upon the people that are gathered out of the nations, *which have gotten cattle and goods, and dwell in the midst of the land."* Concerning which occurrences, it is expressly stated at verse 16 : " It shall be *in the latter days."*

From this it is evident that it is the object of the invader to take possession of a flourishing but unarmed agricultural colony recently developed in the land of Israel, " which," says the prophecy, speaking retrospectively from the latter-day point of observation, " hath been *always* waste, but is now brought forth." " A desolate place now inhabited," is the description put into the mouth of Gog at the time of the invasion (verse 12), which shows the land of Israel to have been recently recovered from desolation, but not to have reached a self-protecting position.

This suggests a question, to which we indirectly obtain an answer in the same chapter : How comes it, in the face of armed military nations, that Israel should re-establish themselves in their desolate mountains, without armament to protect their newly - acquired prosperity ? To what power do they trust in this " dwelling at rest," " having neither bars nor gates?" The answer is seen in the challenge thrown in the face of the Gogian invader, when he enters the land (verse 13): " Sheba and Dedan, and *the merchants of* TARSHISH, and all the young lions thereof shall say unto thee, Art thou come to take a spoil ? Hast thou gathered thy company to take a prey ? " Here is a power that steps forth as the latter-day defender of Israel, under whose protection, the newly-established settlement on the mountains of Israel had been developed. Is it possible to identify this description with any modern power ? A conclusive mode of reasoning identifies it with Britain. The evidence is collected in an anonymous work, entitled *The Kings of the East,* and published in 1842. The evidence is not well digested in that work ; we give the pith of it in our own way.

The first fact to be looked at is the one stated in Ezek. xxvii. 12, that Tarshish was a *merchant of Tyre* (ancient Phœnicia), supplying the Tyrian market with "silver, iron, tin and lead." If the source of the supply of these metals to the Tyrian market can be ascertained, the Scripture Tarshish is discovered.

It is a fact that tin was universally used by the ancients as the alloy for the hardening of copper, in the making of swords and other implements. It is another fact that none of the ancient civilised countries possessed tin mines. It is another fact that till the destruction of Tyre by Alexander, all countries were supplied by the market of Tyre, and that the source of the Tyrian supply was, till that time, a secret. The secret was afterwards open to the Greeks and Romans, who went to the same source of supply. What source was that? The answer derivable from Strabo, Herodotus, and other ancient historians, is that the Greeks and Romans, like the Phœnicians before them, went for tin to the islands known as the "Cassiterides."

What does "Cassiterides" mean? The tin islands, from *cassiteros*—the name given by the Greeks to tin. Look on any ancient map, and Cassiterides will be found marked under the British Islands. But originally the Greeks did not know the name by which the *Cassiterides* were known to the original Phœnician traders. They only knew there were such islands without knowing where, or what geographical phrase they were known by. When they did know, they found they were known as the Britannic Isles. Why *Britannic* isles?

Britannia is a Celtic name. The Celtic language is Phœnician naturalised in these islands from the first settlers, the descendants of Tarshish, son of Javan, one of those by whom "the isles of the Gentiles were divided in their lands."—(Gen. x. 5.) In pure Celtic, Britannia signifies the LAND OF METALS; in Syriac, from which it is derived, *Baratanac* means the land of tin. The modern name, Britain, is but a modification of the ancient Baratanac or Britannia, consequently, *The British Isles* literally mean the tin isles, and identify Britain as the Cassiterides (tin islands) of the Greeks, and the Tarshish of the Scriptures which supplied Tyre with "silver, iron, tin and lead."

In addition to the evidence of historians that Tyre drew her mineral supplies from certain northern islands beyond the pillars of Hercules (the Straits of Gibraltar), there is abundant evidence in Cornwall and the south and west coasts of Ireland, of the existence of ancient mineral mines worked by Phœnician enterprise. Not only are numerous exhausted tin mines found in various localities, whose history is totally unknown, but implements of Phœnician workmanship are found abundantly. Messrs. Lysons, in their account of Cornwall (page 204), say: " Cornwall has been celebrated for its tin mines from very remote antiquity. We learn from Strabo, Herodotus, and other ancient writers, that the Phœnicians, and after them the Greeks and Romans, traded for tin to Cornwall, under the name of the Cassiterides, from a very early period. Diodorus Siculus, who wrote in the reign of Augustus, gives a particular description of the manner in which the valuable metal was dug and prepared by the Britons." Fragments of ancient weapons are frequently discovered in Cornwall, in streams and buried in the ground. Messrs. Lysons, in the book already quoted, say, " they are instruments of mixed metal, commonly called celts, apparently cast in imitation of the stone hatchets and chisels of the early inhabitants. They are found in greater abundance in Cornwall than in any other part of the kingdom . . . Several were found on the side of Karnbri Hill, in the year 1844. In the parish of Halant, four miles north of St. Michael's Mount, in the year 1802, a farmer discovered, about two feet below the surface of the earth, a quantity of celts, weighing about 14 to 15 pounds, with pieces of copper swords and heavy lumps of fine copper . . . Another large quantity of celts, with spear heads and broken pieces of copper swords, with several lumps of metal, weighing altogether about 80 pounds, was discovered in the parish of St. Hilary, about the year 1800." Other similar discoveries have been made, and a comparison of these ancient relics with the armour described by Homer in the *Iliad*, as worn by the Greeks (who were supplied by Tyre), shows they are identical in metal and manufacture. As regards Ireland, a report on the metallic mines of Leinster was presented to the Royal Dublin Society in 1828, in which the following paragraph occurs : " If we may judge from the number of ancient mine excavations which are still visible in almost every part of Ireland, it would appear that an ardent spirit for mining adventure must have pervaded this country at some very remote period . . Many of our mining excavations exhibit appearances *similar to the surface workings of the most ancient mines of Cornwall, which are generally attributed to the Phœnicians."* M. Moore, in his first volume of the *History of Ireland*, says: " Numbers of swords made of brass, have been found in different parts of the country . . . It has been thought not improbable that all these weapons, the Irish as well as the others, were of the same Punic or

Phœnician origin, and may be traced to those colonies on the coast of Spain which traded anciently with the British Isles." The Rev. Dr. Vincent, in his treatise on the commerce and navigation of the ancients in the Indian Ocean, says: "Tin is mentioned as an import into Africa, Arabia, Scindi and the coast of Malabar. It has continued an article of commerce, BROUGHT OUT OF BRITAIN IN ALL AGES, and *conveyed to all the countries in the Mediterranean by the Phœnicians*, Greeks and Romans, and carried into the Eastern Ocean from the origin of commerce."

There were two places called Tarshish—the one in the east, the other in the west. This is evident from the fact that the ships of Solomon, built at Ezion-geber, went to Tarshish, bringing, once in three years, "gold and silver, ivory, apes and peacocks" (1 Kings x. 22); while Jonah, in attempting to escape the presence of the Lord, shipped at Joppa (modern Jaffa) to go to a place of the same name.— (Jonah i. 3.) Now Joppa is in the Mediterranean and Ezion-geber is in the Red Sea; and as the passage round the Cape of Good Hope was unknown, it follows there was a Tarshish in the east and a Tarshish in the west—probably owing to their both springing from the same family of colonists—the descendants of Tarshish, the grandson of Japheth. The western Tarshish produced "silver, iron, tin, and lead;" the eastern, "gold and silver, ivory, apes and peacocks." The products of the first point to Britain, the undoubted Baratanac of the Phœnicians, and Cassiterides of the Greeks; and the products of the second (considered in connection with the length of time occupied by the voyage), point to India. It requires but to be mentioned that both realms are in our day *united under British sovereignty*, which also holds Gibraltar in Spain, a midway station corresponding to the ancient Gadir, or Tartessus (Cadiz), which some, on insufficient grounds, think to be Tarshish. The position of Britain thus covers the whole of the area to which the name of Tarshish can be applied.

It may seem a difficulty that the name Tarshish should have been so entirely lost in connection with Britain. It must be remembered, however, that the names in Hebrew, by which the lands and nations are spoken of in the Scriptures, rarely resemble those by which they were known to the inhabitants of those countries themselves: and as it is by the latter names that they become known to profane writers, and perpetuated in history, it is no marvel that there should be a discrepancy between the nomenclature of Scripture and the nomenclature of the nations. The identification of them is more dependent upon facts than resemblance in sound.

The facts of the case are in a nutshell. It is testified that Tarshish supplied Tyre (the Phenice of profane writers) with "silver, iron, lead and tin." It is demonstrated that these supplies came from Baratanac (the isles of tin), softened in the course of ages into Britain. The conclusion follows that the Bible Tarshish is Britain.

The conclusion is made certain by the position of Britain. Tarshish is described as "the merchants of Tarshish and all the young lions thereof." Britain is the mercantile power of the world; she is to the modern world what Tyre, her ancestor, was to the ancient world. Again, Tarshish in the latter day, is described as the possessor of ships; "the ships of Tarshish" (Is. ii. 16): and, behold, Britain has more ships than all the other nations put together. "The young lions thereof" agrees with the heraldry of British Power. "The ships of Tarshish" is another phrase by which she is characterised in Isaiah lx. 8, in connection with the time of Israel's restoration—a phrase applicable to Britain alone as a characteristic description: for she rules the seas, and her ships outnumber those of all other nations put together. Some have broached the idea that Tarshish was the ancient Tartessus in Spain (the modern Cadiz); but there is little to favour that idea beyond a superficial resemblance in the name, while there is the fact that Tartessus was made use of as a port of call by the ships trading between the tin islands and Tyre. The ancient Tartessus has disappeared from the historic arena, while the song of the tin islands ("Rule *Britannia*,") is heard throughout the world.

"Sheba and Dedan (districts in Southern Arabia, anciently so called, indirectly subject to the British Crown), and the merchants of Tarshish and the young lions thereof," is, without doubt, the prophetic description of the wide-shadowing power of Britain in the latter days, whence it follows that Britain is the latter-day protector of the Jews against the Russo-European attempt that will be made (for political reasons) to take possession of their flourishing colony to be established in the land of Israel.

CHAPTER VII.

Britain's latter day friendship for the Jews—The Scripture testimony on the subject—The human cause of that friendship, and of England's antagonism to Russia—The British Empire in India—Britain's communications through Asiatic Turkey—Purchase of the Suez Canal, and coming British occupation of Egypt and Syria—Current schemes for Jewish settlement in Palestine—The Montefiore Testimonial—Jewish views on the subject—A Jew at the head of the British Government.

THE evidence of Britain's latter-day friendship for the Jews is not confined to the passage quoted from Ezekiel. Isaiah plainly speaks of it. Referring to the day when "The Redeemer shall come to Zion," which Paul quotes as an unaccomplished prophecy in his day, and which therefore relates to the second coming of Christ—(Acts i. 11; Heb. ix. 28; 1 Pet. v. 4),—Jehovah, by the prophet, thus addresses Israel: "Arise, shine, for thy light is come, and the glory of the Lord is risen upon thee. For, behold the darkness shall cover the earth, and gross darkness the people. But the Lord shall arise upon thee, and His glory shall be seen upon thee, and the Gentiles shall come to thy light and kings to the brightness of thy rising . . . Surely THE ISLES shall wait for me, and *the ships of Tarshish first,* to bring thy sons from far and thy daughters from the ends of the earth"—(Isaiah lx. 1-3, 9). Again, in Isaiah xviii. we meet with the following address to a land in the latter days "shadowing with wings," or exercising a widely-extended imperial jurisdiction, which is the case with Britain only. The land is described as one that "sendeth her ambassadors by the sea," which shows that it is in an insular situation as Britain, and no other country is. Other nations send ambassadors by land, but England is obliged to use the sea. Her ambassadors are said, in the English version, to go "in vessels of bulrushes," but this, it is agreed by several eminent Hebraists, ought to be "vessels of turning things," or whirling things—a distinct allusion to the invention of steamships. "Vessels of bulrushes" would be useless on the ocean, though they may suit the smooth water of the Nile. The next sentence in the passage settles the point, "Go, ye *swift* messengers:" this is a suitable description of Britain's steam vessels, and not of Egyptian boats of papyrus. Well, on what errand are "the swift messengers" to be sent? "Go, ye swift messengers, to a nation scattered and peeled, to a people terrible from their beginning hitherto: a nation meted out and trodden down, whose land the rivers (military powers) have spoiled." The scattered nation whose land has been destroyed, is the Jewish nation. What is the object of this mission of the steamships of Tarshish to the scattered nation? The answer is in verse 7 of the chapter: "In that time shall the present be brought unto the Lord of Hosts, of a people scattered and peeled, . . . to the place of the name of the Lord of Hosts, the Mount Zion "— (Isaiah xviii. 7). In short, Britain's ships are destined to be employed in the work of gathering the Jews from all parts of the world. But this not until the divine interference that follows the Russian attempt to wrest the infant "Judaic" colony from the hands of Britain.

What is it, as regards the human exigencies of the case, that leads England to be friendly to the Jews, and antagonistic to Russia? The answer has been displayed in a thousand newspapers, and resounded from a thousand public platforms during the past twelve months. The possession of India by England, and the determination of all classes of Englishmen that India shall remain in English possession, is the soul and marrow of England's policy on the Eastern question. If England did not possess India, the fate of Turkey would be as immaterial to England as the cession of Nice and Savoy to France. But she possesses India; and her communications with India lie through the Turkish empire. These communications are safe so long as the Sultan of Constantinople is lord of the empire, but let Turkey fall, and there is nothing to interpose a barrier between these communications and the might of the Russian colossus which presses southward both in Europe and Asia with irresistible gravitation. It is the fear that Russia would, in such a case, ultimately become strong for aggression in India, that inspires English statesmen of all parties with such a supreme interest in the fate of the Turks and the countries in Turkish possession. It is this which has originated what is known as "the traditional policy of the foreign office," in favour of the maintenance of the independence and integrity of the Ottoman empire. This policy has been abandoned under the pressure of events, and Turkey is likely to be left to her fate at the hand of Russia. But nothing can destroy the necessity for England preserving her Indian communications. Hence, if the worst befall Turkey, England is bound, in the interests of self-preservation, to secure ascendancy in the Asiatic part of the Turkish empire. The purchase of the Suez Canal is a step in this direction. Prophecy reveals another in her coming patronage of the Jewish colonization of Palestine.

Four hundred years ago, there was nothing to give England that connection with Bible lands which she was destined to sustain in the time of the end. The conquest of India was the great event in providence that has brought her into this connection, and will yet develop it more distinctly. So long as Turkey was quiet and safe from aggression, there was no need for overt steps on the part of Britain to establish herself in Egypt and Syria. Turkey was a sufficient barrier between Russia and her Indian communications; but now that the existence of Turkey is imperilled, England is roused to definite action, and in the event of the dismemberment of the Ottoman empire, must add the occupation of Egypt and Syria to the purchase of the Suez Canal. The tendency of events is therefore visibly in the direction foreshown in the sure word of prophecy.

That England will occupy Egypt, and that Egypt will be wrested from her hands by Russian armies, results from several intimations in this "sure word of prophecy." We have already seen that Britain is the power mentioned in Ezek. xxxviii. 13, as the antagonist of the Russo-German invader of Palestine, in the latter days, under the name of "the merchants of Tarshish and all the young lions thereof." According to Daniel xi., in the words already quoted, this northern invader prevails against all opposition, and therefore, against the opposition of the Anglo-Tarshish merchant-power, up to a certain point. The countries, "Edom and Moab and the chief of the children of Ammon," remain in the hands of Gog's Tarshish opponents (Dan. xi. 41); but "the land of Egypt shall not escape" (verse 42), implying that the land of Egypt is, in the first instance, in the hands of the possessor of Edom and Moab, namely Tarshish or Britain. This view is confirmed by a peculiar expression in Isaiah xliii. 3. Referring to the future deliverance of Israel, when it will be said to the south, "Give up," and to the north, "Keep not back," Jehovah says, "I gave Egypt for thy ransom, Ethiopia and Seba for thee."—(Isaiah xliii. 3) This implies that the transferring of Egypt to some power, brings about or is connected with the ransom of Israel in its preliminary stage. Egypt was given as "wages" to Nebuchadnezzar twenty-five centuries ago, for his service as Jehovah's instrument against Tyrus (Ezek. xxix. 18, 19), without Nebuchadnezzar knowing either that he served God in the matter of Tyrus, or that he got Egypt for a recompense. So Britain will receive

Egypt as the price of Israel's deliverance, without either the deliverance 'or the payment of the ransom appearing in any other light than as a natural transaction, except to those who look at the affairs of nations from a divine stand-point. The possession of Egypt has become a political necessity to England, for the reasons already mentioned; and the preservation of her footing in Egypt, particularly in defence of the Suez Canal, by the interposition of a territorial buffer between that canal and Russian advances from the Caucasus, leads, in the arrangement of the Eastern Question, to her occupation of the Holy Land and the settlement of Israel there.

Already, numerous schemes exist for the re-settlement of Palestine by Jews; and one of them has assumed practical and organic shape, in the form of a testimonial to Sir Moses Montefiore, who requested that the testimonial should take the form of a plan for improving the condition of the Jews of Palestine. A gentleman has been appointed as the committee's agent in the execution of the scheme; but, for the present, during the uncertainties of the Eastern Question, the scheme is in abeyance. If the upshot of the present crisis should be, as is more than probable, the overthrow of the Turkish Empire, the way will be open for the development of this scheme to an indefinite extent. The one great barrier in the way of all such schemes, hitherto, has been the uncertainty of life and property in Syria under the Turkish Government. Under British protection, this state of uncertainty would soon vanish, and the formation of a Jewish settlement on the scale required by prophecy, would be a matter of a very few years. The agitation of · the Montefiore scheme has disposed the minds of thousands of the race of Israel throughout the world, to return to their land as soon a sa scheme for that purpose is sufficiently matured. In Roumania, the Jews are being expelled from whole districts, and would gladly avail themselves of such an opportunity.

The minds of the superior class of Jews are also exercised in the same direction, but from another point of view. This is signally illustrated in George Eliot's new work, *Deronda*, in which a Jew is made to express himself in the following manner :—

"What wonder that multitudes of our people are ignorant, narrow, superstitious ? What wonder ? What wonder ? The night is unto them, they have no vision; in their darkness they are unable to divine; the sun is gone down over the prophets, and the day is dark above them; their observances are as nameless relics. . .
Revive the organic centre: let the unity of Israel which has made the growth and form of its religion, be an outward reality. Looking towards a land and a polity, our dispersed people in all the ends of the earth may share the dignity of a national life, which has a voice among the peoples of the East and the West—which will

plant the wisdom and skill of our race so that it may be, as of old, a medium of transmission and understanding. Let that come to pass, and the living warmth will spread to the weak extremities of Israel, and superstition will vanish, not in the lawlessness of the renegade, but in the illumination of great facts which widen feeling, and make all knowledge alive as the young offspring of beloved memories.

· · · · · ·

"I say that the effect of our separateness will not be completed and have its highest transformation, unless our race takes on again the character of a nationality. That is the fulfilment of the religious trust that moulded them into a people, whose life has made half the inspiration of the world. What is it to me that the ten tribes are lost untraceably, or that multitudes of the children of Judah have mixed themselves with the Gentile populations as a river with rivers ? Behold our people still ! Their skirts spread afar ; they are torn and soiled and trodden on ; but there is a jewelled breast-plate. Let the wealthy men, the monarchs of commerce, the learned in all knowledge, the skilful in all arts, the speakers, the political councillors, who carry in their veins the Hebrew blood which has maintained its vigour in all climates, and the pliancy of the Hebrew genius for which difficulty means new device—let them say, 'We will lift up a standard, we will unite in a labour hard but glorious, like that of Moses and Ezra, a labour which shall be a worthy fruit of the long anguish whereby our fathers maintained their separateness, refusing the ease of falsehood.' They have wealth enough to redeem the soil from debauched and paupered conquerors ; they have the skill of the statesman to devise, the tongue of the orator to persuade."

The *Hebrew Observer* has also delivered itself on the same subject as follows :—

"Is there no other destiny for Palestine but to remain a desert, or to become the appendage of an ambitious foreign power? Syria will ere long be the *entrepot* between the East and the West. On the Euphrates and along the coast, old cities will revive and new ones will be built ; the old times will come back on a scale of greater vastness and splendour ; and bridging the level districts, the steam car will run in the track of the caravan. Syria, then, will be a place of trade—pre-eminently. And who are pre-eminently the traders of the world ? Will there, when the coming change takes place, be any more congenial field for the energies of the Jew? The country wants capital and population. The Jews can give it both. And has not England a special interest in promoting such a restoration ? Russia covets Syria, and desires to have a Greek patriarch supreme at Jerusalem. It would be a blow to England if either of her great rivals got hold of Syria. Her empire, reaching from Canada in the West to Calcutta and Australia in the South-east, would be cut in two. England does not covet new territories, but she must see they do not get into the hands of her rival Powers. She must preserve Syria to herself through the Syrians. Does not policy, then—if that were all—exhort England to foster the nationality of the Jews, and aid them, as opportunity may offer, to return as a leavening power to their old country? Rome has persecuted the Jews. Nowhere has oppression and contempt attended the Jews so much as in Rome, in the despised Ghetto quarter of the Eternal-City. Russia, too, in her Greek orthodoxy, condemns the Jew. But in England he is unfrowned on by the Church, and endowed with the fullest rights of citizen. England, also, is the great maritime power of the world. To England, then, naturally belongs the rôle favouring the settlement of the Jews in Syria. Do not the dictates of policy exhort her to the same course? The nationality of the Jews exists: the spirit is there, and has been for three thousand years ; but the external form, the crowning bond of union, is still wanting. A nation must have a country. And is not Syria open to them? They seized it of yore, as a wave of armed and enthusiastic warriors ; will they not, ere long, return to it as pioneers of civilization to re-clothe the land with fertility, and as the busy agents of a commerce which will bring together both East and West on the neck of land between the Euphrates and the Levant ? The old land and the old people, and commerce flowing again in its old channels. We see strange things now-a-days ; may not this also be one of the notable sights of this epoch of resurrection ? "

All these circumstances indicate a preparation for the work of Jewish revival as soon as the way is open. Nor can it be forgotten that Lord Beaconsfield, the disposer of British power at the present moment, is a Jew, who in his works before the world, has given strong evidence of his " Judaic sympathies " in general, and his predisposition to Jewish restoration in particular. That such a man, at such a time, should hold the reins of government in the nation to which is prophetically assigned the work of befriending the Jews in the time of the end, cannot but be looked upon as something more than an interesting circumstance.

CHAPTER VIII.

Dismemberment of the Turkish Empire—A peaceful interval—Russian attack upon Syria in British occupation—Defeat of the British forces and Russian seizure of North Palestine and Egypt—Christ's arrival on the Scene—Violent overthrow of the invader, and destruction of the British fleet—The object of these mighty events and their sequel.

THE break-up of the Turkish empire, as before stated, will compel England to secure her footing in Asiatic Turkey, for the protection of India ; and all things seem to be working together to lead her to favour the Jewish re-settlement of Palestine, with a view to that end. Turkey overthrown and dismembered, then will probably ensue a brief respite in the march of events, during which this work of re-settlement goes forward. This peaceful interval is closed by a renewal of the jealousies belonging inherently to the incompatible interests of Russia and England. The fermentation ends in war. Russia and the many people with her come "like a storm" upon Syria, hoping to replenish an exhausted exchequer by the riches of a thriving Jewish colony, and at the same time, intent upon advancing on British communications with India, with a view to the overthrow of the British supremacy which is such an offence to the ambitions of military Europe. The invasion is successful. Syria is occupied and Egypt over-run ;

Jerusalem taken after a siege, and the remnant of the broken forces of Britain brought to bay in Edom and Moab, the south eastern corner of the Holy Land.

Russia and her confederates are on the point of achieving the dominion of the world, when a power appears on the scene, alike unexpected by Russia and England. Christ arrives on the scene, invisibly to the enemies' forces. The crash of heaven's artillery startles the assembled nations of the world : panic throws them into confusion; the rage of the elements decimates the struggling thousands. Fire from heaven, the hot thunderbolt, bituminous burning rain, make short work of the multitudinous and embattled foe, and drive a miserable remnant, amounting to a sixth, out of the country, pursued by a handful of Jewish soldiers, acting under the orders of a new and unknown leadership. These facts are stated in the following prophetic testimonies :—

"And it shall come to pass at the same time when Gog shall come against the land of Israel, saith the Lord God, that my fury shall come up in my face. For in my jealousy and in the fire of my wrath have I spoken, surely in that day there shall be a great shaking in the land of Israel: so that the fishes of the sea, and the fowls of the air, and the beasts of the field, and the creeping things that creep upon the earth, and all the men that are upon the face of the earth shall shake at MY PRESENCE, and the mountains shall be thrown down and the steep places shall fall; and every wall shall fall to the ground. And I will call for a sword against him throughout all my mountains, saith the Lord God; every man's sword shall be against his brother. And I will plead against him with pestilence and with blood; and I will rain upon him and upon his bands, and upon the many people that are with him, and overflowing rain and great hailstones, fire and brimstone."— (Ezek. xxxviii. 18-22).

" And I will turn thee back and will leave but the sixth part of thee, and will cause thee to come out of the north parts, and will bring thee upon the mountains of Israel. And I will smite thy bow out of thy left hand, and will cause thine arrows to fall out of thy right hand. Thou shalt fall upon the mountains of Israel, thou and all thy bands and the people that is with thee; I will give thee unto the ravenous birds of every sort, and to the beasts of the field to be devoured. Thou shalt fall upon the open fields, for I have spoken it, saith the Lord God."—(Ezek. xxxix. 2-5.)

" Then shall the Lord go forth and fight against those nations as he fought in the day of battle. And his feet shall stand on that day on the Mount o. Olives which is before Jerusalem on the east, and the Mount of Olives shall cleave in the midst thereof, toward the east and toward the west, and there shall be a great valley; and half of the mountain shall remove toward the north and half toward the south. And ye shall flee to the valley of the mountains; for the valley of the mountains shall reach unto Azal; yea, ye shall flee like as ye fled from before the earthquake in the days of Uzziah, King of Judah; and the Lord my God shall come, and all the saints with thee . . . And this shall be the plague wherewith the Lord shall smite the people that have fought against Jerusalem. Their flesh shall consume away whilst they stand upon their feet, and their eyes shall consume away in their holes, and their tongue shall consume away in their mouth. And it shall come to pass in that day that a great tumult from the Lord shall be among them; and they shall lay hold everyone on the hand of his neighbour, and his hand shall rise up against the hand of his neighbour."—(Zech. xiv. 3-5; 12, 13.)

" Let the nations be awakened and come up the valley of Jehoshaphat: for there will I sit to judge all the heathen round about. Put ye in the sickle: for the harvest is ripe; come, get you down, for the press is full, the fats overflow; for their wickedness is great. Multitudes, multitudes in the valley of decision; for the day of the Lord is near in the valley of decision. The sun and moon shall be darkened and the stars shall withdraw their shining. The Lord shall roar out of Zion and utter His voice from Jerusalem; and the heavens and the earth shall shake; but the Lord shall be the hope of his people and the strength of the children of Israel."—(Joel iii. 12-16.)

" Come near, all ye nations to hear, and hearken, ye people; let the earth hear, and all that is therein; the world and all things that come forth of it. For the indignation of the Lord is upon all nations, and his fury upon all their armies; He hath utterly destroyed them; He hath delivered them to the slaughter. Their slain also shall be cast out and their stink shall come up out of their carcases, and the mountains shall melt with their blood . . For it is the day of the Lord's vengeance, and the year of recompenses for the controversy of Zion."—(Isaiah xxxiv. 1-3, 8.)

"And I saw an angel standing in the sun; and he cried with a loud voice saying to all the fowls that fly in the midst of heaven, Come and gather yourselves together unto the supper of the Great God: that ye may eat the flesh of kings and the flesh of captains, and the flesh of mighty men, and the flesh of horses and of them that sit on them, and the flesh of all men, both free and bond, both small and great. And I saw the beast, and the kings of the earth and their armies, gathered together to make war against him that sat on the horse, and against his army. And the beast was taken, and with him the false prophet that wrought miracles before him, with which he deceived them that had the mark of the beast, and them that worshipped his image. These both were cast alive into a lake of fire burning with brimstone. And the remnant were slain with the sword of him that sat upon the white horse, which sword proceeded out of his mouth: and all the fowls were filled with their flesh." (Rev. xix. 17-21).

The object of the cataclysm is similar to that of the plagues of Egypt. The object of these is thus stated: " *That thou mightest know that the Lord He is God;* there is none else beside Him."—(Deut. iv. 35.) The object of the Armageddon overthrow is thus defined: " I will bring thee, O Gog, against my land, THAT THE HEATHEN (*goyim*, nations) MAY KNOW ME when I shall be sanctified in thee before their eyes . . . Thus will I magnify myself and sanctify myself, and *I will be known in the the eyes of many nations, and they shall know that I am Jehovah.*"—(Ezek. xxxviii. 16, 23.) " All the nations shall see *the judgment that I have executed and the hand that I have laid upon them.*"—(xxxix. 21.) It is a long time since God made the visible interposition which wrote His name in the nation of Israel. In the lapse of time, the impression has almost faded, and it is to be renewed with terrible deeds of judgment; as he saith by Isaiah: " For a long time I have holden my peace; I have been still and refrained myself. Now will I cry like a travailing woman. I will destroy and devour at once."—(Isaiah xlii. 14.)

Will British power escape the blow that is intended to level all human pride in the dust? Not so: "The day of the Lord of Hosts shall be upon everyone that is proud and lofty and upon everyone that is lifted up, and he shall be brought low . . ; and upon all THE SHIPS OF TARSHISH, and upon all pleasant pictures. And the loftiness of man shall be bowed down, and the haughtiness of men shall be made low, and the Lord alone shall be exalted in that day."— (Isaiah ii. 12, 17.) This specific allusion to the ships of Tarshish— the navy of Great Britain, which · is the pride and power of the country—would indicate that it shares in the disaster that shatters the northern league. The form of the disaster seems to be hinted at in another prophecy, which is couched in the language of accomplished fact—a common peculiarity in Bible prophecy: "Lo, the kings were assembled; they passed by together. They saw; so they marvelled; they were troubled, so they hasted away. Fear took hold upon them there and pain as of a woman in travail. *Thou breakest* THE SHIPS OF TARSHISH *with an east wind.*—(Psalm xlviii. 4-7.) From this it would appear that the outburst of elemental power that scatters the hosts of Gog, extends also to the neighbouring Mediterranean, and involves the British fleet in the common destruction.

This is but the commencement of "the great day of the Lord." What follows? The subsequent re-establishment of the kingdom of Israel in the hands of the long-rejected but then newly-arrived King of the Jews, who retains in his hands the marks of crucifixion, which he exhibits to the Jews in proof of his identity, with the result of inducing a great and national mourning for their past crimes (Zech. xii. 10-14); and Christ's subsequent call to the governments of the world to surrender to him, which will engage our attention in another chapter.

I<small>T</small> has been sufficiently apparent that the events of "the latter days" involve peculiarly the fortunes of the Jewish nation. This is so essential a feature of the latter day situation, that the angel who came to reveal the whole course of events to Daniel, said to him, " I am come to make thee understand *what shall befall thy people in the latter days*."—(Dan. x. 14.) The political occurrences of former days had to do with God's nation, when the men having to do with them knew nothing about it. Thus we read in Isa. xliii. 14 : "*For your sakes*, I have sent to Babylon and brought down all their nobles." That the affairs of men should be divinely manipulated with Jewish objects is a view repugnant to the common run of men : they look upon the Jews as a contemptible and effete race, whose part in history is played. Apart from revelation, no doubt this is a natural view ; but in view of the purpose of God as revealed by the prophets, it is one that will be rejected by those who believe what Paul states in Heb. i. 1 : " God at sundry times and in divers manners, *spake unto the fathers by the prophets*." The Gentile view of the case and the purpose of God are brought into juxtaposition in Micah iv. 11 : "Many nations are gathered against thee (Israel), saying, Let her be defiled; let our eyes look upon Zion. *But they know not the thoughts of the Lord, neither understand they His counsel :* for he shall gather them (the nations) as the sheaves unto the floor. Arise and thresh, O daughter of Zion, for I will make thy horn iron and thy hoofs brass, and thou shalt beat in pieces many people."

One of the very objects of the gathering of the nations to Armageddon, is thus expressed in Joel iii. : " I will gather all nations, and bring them down into the valley of Jehoshaphat, *and will plead with them there for my people and for my heritage, Israel,* whom they have scattered amongst the nations and parted my land." The nations have a responsibility to discharge for their treatment of the Jews, and the discharging of it will involve a time of trouble such as never was since there was a nation upon earth—(Dan. xii. 1). A feature of this time of trouble will be that the Jews will be made use of to follow up the divine stroke of Armageddon, in the process of subjugating the whole earth to the sceptre of the king of the Jews. Thus it is testified: "Thou art my battleaxe and weapons of war; with thee (Israel) will I break in pieces the nations; with thee will I destroy kingdoms" (Jer. li. 20); and also: "The remnant of Jacob shall be among the Gentiles in the midst of many people as a lion among the beasts of the forest, and as a young lion among the flocks of sheep, who, if he go through, both treadeth down and breaketh in pieces" (Mich. v. 8).

Who are these Jews, who occupy such a prominent position in the latter-day work of God, even as they did in the work of old? The answer is to be read in the words addressed by Moses to the children of Israel after the exodus from Egypt: "The Lord thy God hath chosen thee to be *a special people unto himself* above all people that are on the face of the earth"—(Deut. vii. 6). The Jews are therefore God's nation on the earth. Ay, but say some, they are cast off. But why? Hearken to the word of God by Amos: "*You only have I known* of all the families of the earth: *therefore* I will punish you for all your iniquity." Israel's cast-off state in punishment of her sins, is therefore evidence that they are the people of divine choice and destiny. Are they to remain cast-off for ever? Let the same word answer the question. "I will gather her that is driven out and her that I have afflicted, and I will make her that halted a preserved people, and her *that was cast far off* A STRONG NATION"—(Mich. iv. 6). "I will bring them again to place them; for I have mercy upon them, and *they shall be as though I had not cast them off*"—(Zech. x. 6). But you say, they are a bad and disobedient race. Never mind: God has chosen them; and this is a sufficient reason for our recognition of them in their true character. Remember David's treatment of an evil Saul, because he was "the Lord's anointed."—(1 Sam. xxvi. 11.) Ponder also this solemn reproof of a contrary mind: "Considerest thou not what this people have spoken, saying, The two families which the Lord hath chosen, He hath even cast them off. Thus they have despised my people, that they should be no more a nation before them. Thus saith the Lord, If my covenant be not with day and night, and If I have not appointed the ordinances of heaven and earth, then will I cast away the seed of Jacob."—(Jer. xxxiii. 24; also xxxi. 37.) Anyone desiring further evidence of God's purpose to restore Israel to their land may consult the following Scriptures:—Isaiah xi. 11-12; xlix. 18 to the end; Ezek. xxxvii. 21 to the end; xxxix. 21 to the end; and on a reading of the prophets, the earnest and attentive reader will find many other such like declarations, throwing light on the expectation of the disciples of Christ, as expressed in their parting question : " Lord, wilt thou at this time restore again the kingdom to Israel? "—(Acts i. 6.)

The Jews in their restoration are to be purified from the evil in their midst: " He shall purify the sons of Levi, and purge them as gold and silver, that they may offer unto the Lord an offering in righteousness. Then shall the offering of Judah and Jerusalem be pleasant unto the Lord as in the days of old, and as in former years."—(Mal. iii. 3.) " I will take away out of thee *them that rejoice in thy pride*; thou shalt no more be haughty because of mine holy mountain. I will also leave in the midst of thee an afflicted and poor people, and they shall trust in the name of the Lord."—(Zeph. iii. 11.) " I will purge out from among you the rebels and them that transgress against me. I will bring them forth out of the countries where they sojourn, and they shall not enter into the land of Israel."—(Ezek. xx. 38.) In view of these testimonies, there is no room for the objection which many feel to the idea of Israel's restoration on the score of their national insubordination to the ways of God. But even if there were not the explanation which there is on this point, the evidence would be conclusive to such as regard the Bible as the Word of God, that the Jews are destined to play an important part in the terrible period that marks the transition from the present constitution of things to the " world to come," or new order of things when "the kingdoms of this world shall have become the kingdoms of our Lord and of his Christ, and he shall reign for ever and ever."—(Rev. xi. 15.)

Previous chapters have shewn them planted in a partial restoration, on the mountains of Israel, as an agricultural and commercial colony under British auspices, when the Turkish empire shall have passed away. We have seen Russian armies descend upon the prospering infant colony, and wrest the country from British hands. We have seen the assembled armies smitten with a divine stroke which drives them out of the country, and leaves but a sixth part. We have seen Britain prostrate by the same power, and Israel abased in the utter-

most depths of national remorse, at the discovery that their deliverer
is the Nazarene whom they have with bitterness rejected in all their
generations. What is the next item in the stupendous programme?
Has the work to be done attained at that stage, the point of com-
pletion? The answer is in harmony with the fitness of things. The
staggering blow inflicted on human power in Palestine, is but the
beginning of a process which is to grind the universal fabric of human
government to pieces. " I will send those that escape of them unto
the nations . . . to the isles afar off that have not
heard of my fame, neither have seen my glory, and they shall declare
my glory among the Gentiles "—(Isa. lxvi. 19). " I will send a fire on
Magog, and among them that dwell carelessly in the isles, and they
shall know that I am the Lord "—(Ezekiel xxxix. 6). A message
goes forth from the Holy Land, " *Fear God and give Him glory*, for
the hour of His judgment is come " (Rev. xiv. 7). " Be wise now,
therefore, O ye kings ; be instructed, ye judges of the earth ; . .
. Kiss the Son, lest he be angry, and ye perish from the way,
when his wrath is kindled but a little"—(Ps. ii. 10-12). " Kings shall
shut their mouths at him for that which had not been told them
shall they see, and that which they had not heard shall they consider "
(Isa. lii. 15).

The shutting of their mouths, on the part of the kings, is the
combined result of consternation at the message which they receive,
and determination to have no parley with the insolent successor of
Mahomet, as they will conceive him to be. With the exception
of Britain, they raise armies against him and assemble to attempt
his overthrow.—(Rev. xix. 19.) The war that ensues is the most
terrible experience of the era. War might be considered impossible
in such a situation of things. That the nations should fight against
Christ may seem incredible, but so was his crucifixion. It is testified
they will fight against him, and that is enough. They are qualified
for the part they have to perform, by the utter misconception that
prevails concerning his future work—a misconception due to a false
theology and ignorance of the Scriptures. They are permitted to
fight that scope may be afforded for those terrible judgments glanced
at in an earlier part of the pamphlet, which are to teach them
righteousness and fit the world for the government of the kingdom
of God. Christ could overthrow the most formidable league of
nations in a moment, with a word of his mouth : but the object in
view precludes this summary exercise of power, as in the case of
Pharaoh, who was allowed to put forth all his power in a series of

acts of resistance, before he was finally submerged in the perdition of the Red Sea. The result, though delayed, is not for a moment doubtful. "The Lamb shall overcome them, for he is King of kings and Lord of lords, and they that are with him are called and chosen and faithful."—(Rev. xvii. 14.)

The power of all Gentile governments vanquished, what follows? "In that day, I will *raise up the tabernacle of David that is fallen, and close up the breaches thereof, and I will raise up his ruins and build it as in the days of old.*"—(Amos ix. 11.) "Of the increase of his (the son of David's) government and peace there shall be no end, *upon the throne of David and upon his kingdom,* to order it and to establish it with justice and with judgment from hence-forth, even for ever.—(Isaiah ix. 8, 9.) "A king (the son of David : see context) shall reign and prosper and execute justice and judgment in the earth. In his days Judah shall be saved, and Israel shall dwell safely.—(Jer. xxiii. 5.) That this is Jesus, is made certain by its New Testament application.—(Luke i. 32 ; Acts ii. 30.) That it will be fulfilled only when Christ has returned, is also certain from his own statements : *e.g.* "When the Son of Man shall sit on the throne of his glory, ye also (my twelve apostles), shall sit with me on twelve thrones, judging the twelve tribes of Israel."—Matt. xix. 28; Luke xxii. 30). When does the Son of Man sit on the throne of his glory? He answers " *When the Son of Man shall come in his glory* and all the holy angels with him, THEN shall he sit on the throne of his glory.—(Matt. xxv. 31.) Hence it is that the appearing and the kingdom of Christ are apostolically associated as in the following instance: "The Lord Jesus Christ shall judge the living and the dead at *his appearing and his kingdom.*"—(2 Tim. iv. 1.) Not only the apostles, but all who, with them, believe on Christ and obey his commandments, will share in "glory to be revealed." "If we suffer with him, we shall REIGN with him "—no empty words—(2 Tim. ii. 12). Of the crown laid up for Paul to be given " at that day," Paul says it will be " not to him only but to *all them also that love his appearing.*"—(2 Tim. iv. 8.) Hence, where this class is dramatically exhibited in the Apocalypse, in their collective completeness, they sing " Thou hast made us unto our God, kings and priests, and we shall reign on the earth."—(Rev. v. 10.) This fact enables us to apprehend the force of Paul's question in impressing on the Corinthian believers the meetness of their settling their own affairs, instead of having recourse to worldly tribunals : " Do ye not know that the saints shall judge the world ?— (1 Cor. vi. 2.)

The prospect opened out in all these testimonies (which are only a few of very many), is that when the present political system is abolished by violence in the impending crisis, it will be replaced by the imperial and absolute authority of David's son and Lord in Jerusalem, and administered in all the earth through his accepted and glorified friends (and who they are may be learnt from Jno. xv. 14). The governing race and nation will be the nation of Israel restored to their land—the first and favoured realm of the empire (Zech. viii. 23 ; Isaiah lx. 12, 15 ; Micah iv. 8 ; Jer. iii. 17 ; Ezekiel xxxvi. 19-38); but all the nations of mankind will rejoice with them in the glories of a reign which will diffuse peace, justice and enlightenment to the end of the earth, and secure that right distribution of earth's abundance, which all human systems of government have failed and must ever fail to accomplish—(Isa. ii. 3 ; Zech. ii. 10-12 ; Ps. lxxii.) At this time only will be realised in its fulness the promise to Abraham, that in him should all the families of the earth be blessed. At this time, also, will the promise of the personal possession of the land be realised, when they shall say " This land that was desolate is become like the garden of Eden " (Ezekiel xxxvi. 35); and when Jehovah has fulfilled the word He has spoken : " Whereas thou (the land of Israel) hast been forsaken and hated so that no man went through thee, I will make thee an eternal excellency, the joy of many generations."—Isaiah lx. 15).

CHAPTER X.

The whole matter brought to a focus—Nebuchadnezzar's vision—The great image of four metals—Daniel's interpretation—A prophetic compendium of universal history—The Prophecy fulfilled—Babylon, Persia, Greece and Rome—The Gothic subversion of the Roman empire—Uprise of the Papacy—The appointed period of its domination expired—Impending perdition of the European body politic—The Eastern Question—The final situation—"Prophecy and the Eastern Question" no fanatical collocation of terms—The divine fiat—The world ripe for judgment—The glorious sequel—All hail the coming day !

In this, the concluding chapter, it will be of advantage to look at the whole matter brought to a focus, in the two visions exhibited with the interpretation, to Daniel, a Jewish captive of the seed royal at the court of Nebuchadnezzar. The common prejudice against the visions of Daniel we may well disregard in view of Christ's allusion to Daniel as a prophet, in whose writings information was to be found as to the events revealed.—(Matt. xxiv. 15): "When ye therefore shall see the abomination of desolation spoken by Daniel the prophet, stand in the holy place *(whoso readeth let him understand")*.

In Daniel ii. we have a vision that is very simple, striking, historically true, and very intelligible, in the scheme and upshot of it. Nebuchadnezzar had a dream. His dream was prefaced by a little contemplation on his part, as he lay in bed before he went to sleep, with regard to the future. He at that time was head of an empire that had carried all before it. Kings were subject to him; and his authority was co-extensive with the civilized world. He naturally wondered what should be after him. God revealed this to him, and here is testified what was revealed. The revelation was imparted at first in the form of a dream, but he could not recall the dream. He summoned the magicians, astrologers, sorcerers, and Chaldeans to be brought before him, to tell him his dream and the interpretation of the dream, threatening death in case they did not do so. They could not supply the information desired, and the decree went forth that they should be slain. Daniel was among the wise men of the king, and also his three companions, Shadrach, Meshach, and Abednego, and they were included in the general edict that the wise men should be slain. Prompted by the natural desire for self-preservation, they that night assembled together in seclusion, and prayed to God that He would divulge this secret to them, that their lives might be saved. Their prayer was answered, and Daniel went next day before the king and said—"The secret which the king hath commanded cannot the wise men, the astrologers, the magicians, the soothsayers, show unto the king;" but, says he, "There is a God in heaven that revealeth secrets and *maketh known to the king Nebuchadnezzar what shall be in the latter days* "—(verse 27, 28). Then he tells his dream.

He says the king saw a great image composed of divers metals: the head of gold, the breast and arms of silver, the belly and thighs of brass, the legs of iron, the feet with the ten toes, part iron and part clay ; and while the king looked at the image, he saw a little stone, cut out of an adjacent mountain without hands, descend with violence upon the feet of the image, as the result of which, the image crumbled to pieces, was reduced to powder, the dust of which was carried away by the wind : and the little stone, gradually enlarging in size, became a great mountain, and filled the whole earth. This was the dream, and he says, "I will show the interpretation: Thou, O king, art a king of kings . . . Thou art this head of gold. And, after thee shall arise another kingdom," not a kingdom in the limited sense of a dominion recognising the sovereignty of a king, but a kingdom in the sense in which the empire of Babylon was a kingdom; that is, an imperial power overshadowing all other nations; "after thee shall arise another kingdom inferior to thee," and, therefore, represented by silver, which is inferior to gold; and after that a third kingdom of brass, represented by the belly and thighs of brass; and, after that, there shall be another kingdom, strong as iron, which shall be greater than the others, inasmuch as he says the iron is stronger than the other metals; but he says, as ye saw clay mixed with the iron towards the feet, so as ye get towards that period of time, the kingdom will be weakened by the introduction of a foreign element. And then he says (verse 44), "*In the days of these kings* SHALL THE GOD OF HEAVEN SET UP A KINGDOM, *which shall never be destroyed,* and the kingdom shall not be left to other people, but it shall break in pieces and consume all these kingdoms, and it shall stand for ever; forasmuch as thou sawest that the stone was cut out of the mountain without hands, and that it brake in pieces the iron, the brass, the clay, the silver and the gold;" as much as to say, "the meaning of the stone descending and destroying the image is, that God will set up a kingdom that will supersede all the human empires that will appear on earth."

Now what do we find in regard to the history thus foreshadowed? We find that it has run in the course marked out up to the present moment. The empire of Babylon was succeeded (before even Daniel had passed off the scene), by the empire of the Medes and Persians. The empire of the Medes and Persians was succeeded by the brazen-coated Greek empire, appropriately represented by the brass of the image. We find that after the lapse of nearly two centuries, the kingdom of the Greeks appeared on the scene, under Alexander the Great, and abolished the empire of the Persians. The empire of the Greeks broke up into four parts after the death of Alexander, as plainly foretold in Dan viii. 22; also xi. 4. This was succeeded by an empire as much stronger than the others as iron is stronger than the other metals; an empire which superseded all the others in everything that can constitute a dominion great. It is proverbial in all history and in all political lessons, that THE ROMAN EMPIRE was the most magnificent political organization that ever exercised authority. The whole civilized world was under its heel; from Rome, on the Tiber, it governed the world in one vast system of universal dominion. But this empire waned in its greatness. It "declined and fell;" as the vision foreshadowed. There would come a time when the iron would be mixed up with clay, and when the iron dominion would be divided into little bits, symbolized by the ten toes. What we see now in Europe is an exemplification of this feature of the symbolism.

It will help the perception of the whole matter to look at a vision that Daniel himself had of the same thing.—(Dan. vii. 2). " I saw in my vision by night, and behold the four winds of the heaven strove upon the great sea. And *four great beasts* came up from the sea, diverse one from another . . . I beheld till the thrones were cast down, and the Ancient of Days did sit, whose garment was white as snow . . . The judgment was set and the books were opened . . . I saw in the night visions, and behold, one like the Son of Man came with the clouds of heaven, and came to the Ancient of Days, and they brought him near before Him. And there was given him dominion, and glory, and a kingdom, that all people, nations, and languages should serve him; his dominion is an everlasting dominion, which shall not pass away, and his kingdom that which shall not be destroyed." Now, what is the meaning of this? We are not left to guess. It is made as plain as we could desire. " These great beasts, which are four, are four kings (or kingdoms), which shall arise out of the earth. But the saints of the Most High shall take the kingdom and possess the kingdom for ever, even for ever and ever "—(verses 17, 18).

In Nebuchadnezzar's vision, after the four metals, came a destroying stone: in this, after the four beasts, came another dominion—the saints of the Most High. But Daniel was struck with the fourth beast, not only on account of its greater size and dreadfulness, but from seeing ten horns in its head, and from noticing another rising up among the ten, and displacing three of them, and exhibiting the peculiarities of eyes and mouth, and speaking loud words. So he asks about it. He says—" Then I would know the truth of the fourth beast, which was diverse from all the others . . . . and of the ten horns that were in his head, and of the others which came up, and before whom three fell; even of that horn that had eyes, and a mouth that spoke very great things. I beheld, and the same horn made war with the saints, and prevailed against them; until the Ancient of Days came, and judgment was given to the saints of the

Most High; and the time came that the saints possessed the kingdom. Thus he said: the fourth beast shall be the fourth kingdom upon earth, which shall be diverse from all kingdoms, and shall devour the whole earth, and shall tread it down, and break it in pieces. And the ten horns out of this kingdom are ten kings that shall arise; (and, therefore, ten kingdoms; for there cannot be ten kings without ten kingdoms;) and another shall arise after them; and he shall be diverse from the first, and he shall subdue three kings. And he shall speak great words against the Most High, and shall wear out the saints of the Most High, and think to change times and laws; and they shall be given into his hand until a time and times and the dividing of time. But the judgment shall sit, and they shall take away his dominion to consume and to destroy it unto the end. And the kingdom and dominion, and the greatness of the kingdom under the whole heaven shall be given to the people of the saints of the Most High, whose kingdom is an everlasting kingdom, and all dominions shall serve and obey Him."

Looking at this in the light of history, what do we see in connection with the Roman empire? That after a prosperous career of about six centuries, the Roman empire was broken up by the irruption from the north of those barbarian hordes, represented by the clay, the Goths, and Huns, and Vandals, and other races of people that inhabited the northern and central countries of Europe and Asia; which came down and upset the Roman Empire. They did not abolish the Roman Empire in the absolute sense, but amalgamated with it after the figure of the clay mixing with iron. They came down and settled in the Roman countries, under Roman civilization, and in many instances co-operating with Roman authority, but ultimately broke up the unity of Roman dominion. This was not the work of a day: the revolution that led to that result extended over a hundred years. It was a long time impending; the Romans for a long time resisted the encroachment of the barbarians, and held them at bay; but at last came the catastrophe; the barriers were thrown down, and the northern flood swept everything before it.

Now what we have to look at is this: that as the final result of their subversion of the Roman Empire, the barbarians divided the Roman Empire substantially into ten political sections The first political settlement of the empire, after the great catastrophe from the north, presents us with a ten-fold division; viz: 1. Vandals; 2. Snevians; 3. Visigoths; 4. Alans; 5. Burgundians; 6. Franks; 7. Hiruli; 8. Huns; 9. Lombards; 10. Ravenna. Machiavelli, the historian of Florence, in the first chapter of his history, gives an enumeration of the kingdoms that rose out of the ruins of the Roman Empire, and the number is ten. Sir Isaac Newton gives the same number, though his mode of enumeration is a little different. We see Daniel's vision verified to that extent, that this fourth empire came to be divided into ten parts, as represented by the ten horns on the head of the beast symbolising it. It would be interesting to bestow a moment's attention on the other little horn that rose after the ten, that had in it eyes and mouth, that supplanted three of the ten, that spoke great words against God, and sought to change times and laws, and that arrogated to itself general authority. Suffice it to say, that one hundred years after the uprise of the ten kingdoms in Roman Europe, the papal power made its appearance, answering to all the peculiarities of the symbol representing it. This power has been more stout in his looks, and more arrogant in his pretensions than the ten, has made war against the saints ; has prevailed against them ; has drenched the soil with their blood ; has spoken great things against God ; has dictated to all the world ; has called himself King of kings and Lord of lords ; has proudly called his city the Eternal City ; has claimed the right to crown the other horns, and even demanded, in token of their subordination to him, that they should kiss his toe. You see it now in the decrepitude required by the fact that the prophetic measurement of his power is up. " Time, times, and the dividing of time," is reducible to 1,260 days, the number of years the Pope has been ecclesiastical lord of men " by law established."

What we have more particularly to mark is, the event which terminates the career of this little horn with eyes and mouth. That event is thus defined in the chapter, first in symbol, then in the plain language of interpretation. THE SYMBOL : " I beheld then, because of the voice of the great words which the horn spake. I beheld, even till the Beast was slain and his body destroyed and given to the burning flame "—(verse 11) *The interpretation :* " The judgment shall sit, and they shall take away his dominion to consume and to destroy it unto the end. And the kingdom and the dominion, and the greatness of the kingdom under the whole heaven, shall be given to the people of the saints of the Most High, whose kingdom is an everlasting kingdom, and all dominions shall serve and obey Him."

Putting the two visions together, they both point to one great climax,—the violent substitution of the authority of God, embodied in Christ and his glorified friends, for the various systems of government that now exist in the world. They illustrate, in a simple and dramatic way, the issues of history as required by the promises made to Abraham and his seed, foretold in the more complex prophecies considered in the earlier parts of this pamphlet. They help us to estimate the Eastern Question in its true character, as the providential development of the situation which has been arranged beforehand, as the appropriate occasion for the accomplishment of God's purpose to bring the world into subjection by judgment, and bless it with a righteous and universal government, in the hands of His glorious Son, enthroned in "the city of the Great King"—Jerusalem, honoured before-time as the seat of a divine government, and again to be chosen as the throne of divine power and glory.—(Jer. iii. 17 ; Zech. ii. 12.)

"Prophecy and the Eastern Question" is no artificial or fanatical collocation of terms. It soberly represents the true character of the times we live in. God has spoken ; centuries ago, He issued the fiat which is complicating European affairs. He decreed the political entanglement which should break up Turkey, decimate the Pope, and bring Russia, with a multitude of people at her steps, to the mountains of Israel, to be broken by Jesus, the King of Israel, preparatory to his re-establishment of the kingdom of David, through which to rule all nations in righteousness for a thousand years. Those who have surrendered themselves to the power of Jehovah's word, "lift up their heads" with quick, instinctive joy, at the accumulating symptoms of the approaching tumult of nations, when "rushing like the rushing of many waters, God shall rebuke them, and they shall flee afar off!"—(Isaiah xvii. 13).

The prospect which fills the world with alarm, generates in Israel's children a glow of triumphant ecstacy. The world cannot understand this. The common run of people lift their hands and eyes with pious horror at the relish with which the scene of coming catastrophe and bloodshed is contemplated by the class believing in prophecy : who appear to them in the light of bloodthirsty war dogs, constantly on the scent for scenes of violence. The world, as of old, calls good evil, and evil good ; darkness light, and light darkness. No doubt, our modern Christians would have objected to the flood, and the destruction of Sodom and Gomorrah, and shuddered at the barbarism of Moses and Joshua in putting women and children to the sword, and the shocking cold-blooded ferocity of Samuel in hewing Agag to pieces. And what would they have said to Jesus, when he rudely overthrew the tables of the money changers in the temple, and expelled them with "a whip of small cords?" They are not Christian at all in the true sense. They are poor effeminate creatures of the flesh, who mistake the feeble impulses of the unenlightened moral sentiments for the divine law. "Cursed be he that doeth the work of the Lord deceitfully, and cursed be he that keepeth back his sword from blood."—(Jer. xlviii. 10).

The world is ripe for divine judgment. The grape-bunches are ready to be reaped for the winepress of God's anger, and the time is near at hand for the WORD OF GOD to come forth to the bloody work of treading out the wicked fruit. With this work, all who are touched with the zeal of the divine service have sympathy; not that they delight in evil, *per se*, but that they have learnt that the stroke of judgment will alone break up the inextricable tangle of evil in which human affairs are, in the present state, involved; that the storm of divine vengeance will alone relieve the atmosphere of the foetid and oppressive elements with which it is charged, and produce health to the nations by the healthy respiration of righteousness and peace; that the relentless arm of righteous retribution—for in righteousness doth he judge and make war—is alone adequate to deal that justice to the peoples which will clear away all encumbrances, and lay the foundation of that state of things in which mankind, first being pure, will be peaceable, filled with goodwill and glory to God.

All hail the coming day! ye have long tarried; break now in glory on our dark horizon, where faith alone, begotten of Yahweh's word, can see the glimmer of thy coming dawn. Oh, we wait with strong desire; give us the first token; send athwart our night the gleaming messenger of thy presence. Release thy prisoners; justify thy children; give them to see with their eyes the unbared arm of Omnipotence lifted up to save His chosen, and to smite all the proud and lofty. Oh, lift the curtain that shuts us out in the darkness which covers all the earth; unveil the impending glory; open the temple; uncover the ark of our covenant with God; scatter the lightnings of Jehovah's anger among the nations. Crash, ye hidden thunders! and destroy them that destroy the earth; bring to the dust the high refuges of rebellion and lies; cast down the thrones; slay the Mother of Harlots; bring perdition on the Fourth Beast; and let all the world know that there is a God who judgeth, and who though long silent, will not always be still, but will rise to avenge His own elect, to carry out His own purpose, and to vindicate His own majesty and honour, against the ignorance, brutishness, perversity and wickedness of a hundred generations. Now shall men see the glory of Yahweh; for His hand is about to be lifted up. The end has come; the times of the Gentiles are knelling to a close. Behold the signs!

CONTENTS.

CHAPTER VII.

CHAPTER VIII.

CHAPTER IX.

CHAPTER X.

www.ingramcontent.com/pod-product-compliance
Lightning Source LLC
Chambersburg PA
CBHW031757090426
42739CB00008B/1056